# MOUNTAINS

## OF THE WORLD

### JOHN CLEARE

Thunder Bay
P·R·E·S·S

ACKNOWLEDGMENTS
In this book I have tried to capture something of this
inspiration, this wonder of mountains. I'm lucky enough
to have climbed and travelled among many of the
world's greater and lesser ranges but by no means
among them all. My photographic coverage is far from
comprehensive; indeed we have selected illustrations
for their pictorial value rather than their geographic
relevance. I'm grateful, therefore, to several of my friends,
particularly to Colin Monteath, that superb Kiwi photographer,
for helping me to widen my coverage of certain areas
and to others for their companionship and patience on the mountain.

All the photographs in this book are from the Mountain Camera collection
and were taken by the author except for the following:
Colin Monteath pages 67, 68/9, 71, 104(B), 105(T and B), 106/7.
John English page 8

COVER, PAGE 1 AND RIGHT: Kumbakarna Himal, Nepal.
*A panorama from the Sinelapha La — the 15,500ft (4,700m)*
*high-level link between the Kangchenjunga glacier, which flows down*
*the northwest flank, and the Yalung glacier which drains the southwest*
*side of Kangchenjunga. A cloud sea covers the Yalung glacier itself but the peaks rise clear*
*into the early evening sky. On the far left is Kangchenjunga South*
*(27,850ft/8,491m), then the summit of Talung peak and the long several-*
*topped crest of Kabru (24,164ft/7,367m) with the pretty cone of*
*Rathong (21,904ft/6,678m) on the right. Collectively this wall*
*of mountains defining the Sikkim frontier is known as the Singalita Ridge.*

First published in the United States by
Thunder Bay Press
5880 Oberlin Avenue, Suite 400
San Diego, CA 92121-9653
1-800-284-3580

Produced by the
Promotional Reprint Company Ltd,
Kiln House, 210 New Kings Road, London SW6 4NZ

# CONTENTS

# INTRODUCTION

Bernese Alps, Switzerland.
*The northern flank of the beautiful Jungfrau (13,642ft/4,158m) rises over the meadows on the slopes of the Lauberhorn above Kleine Scheidegg.*

### GLOSSARY

| | |
|---|---|
| **aiguille** | — *sharp mountain* |
| **arete** | — *narrow ridge* |
| **bergschrund** | — *lateral crevasse on glacier* |
| **breche** | — *(also col)narrow saddle* |
| **couloir** | — *gully* |
| **cwm** | — *(also corrie, cirque)small hanging valley caused by glacier* |
| **gendarme** | — *pinnacle* |
| **moulin** | — *hole in glacier where surface water drains* |
| **mulde** | — *lateral trench along glacier* |
| **neve** | — *upper snow and ice from which a glacier is born* |
| **rognon** | — *rock is land in middle of glacier* |

Mankind has never been indifferent to the mountains which have always appeared on his horizons. Indeed, the high places have usually engendered strong emotions, in less enlightened times often of repulsion, fear or mysticism. For millennia men crossed mountain ranges because they wanted to get to the other side, while bold chamois-hunters and crystal gathers plied their precarious calling below the high peaks. Superstitious mountain peasants, familiar with storm, rock-fall and avalanche, invented appropriate names for the seemingly malevolent mountains among which they lived; witness the Teufelsberg (Devil's Mountain), Monte Dizgratzia (Disaster Mountain), Mont Maudit (Accursed Mountain) and the Eiger (Ogre) of the European Alps.

Early records of more formalised mountain ascents include that of Mount Sinai by Moses and of Kilimanjaro by King Menelik — Sheba's son by Solomon. Inca priests and their sacrificial victims are known to have reached Aconcagua, Ampato and other 20,000ft (6,000m) Andean summits. But these were climbs with an ulterior motive and it is only comparatively recently that mountains have been climbed as an end in themselves, climbed — to repeat Mallory's apocryphal epigram — 'because they are there.'

The history of mountaineering as a sport is an interesting and on-going reflection of the development of European civilisation. The first notable climb for no other reason than to reach the summit is considered to be the ascent in 1492 of Mont Aiguille, an imposing limestone mesa of 6,880ft (2,097m) in the Vercors massif of the French Alps, by Anthoine de Ville and his men on the orders of King Charles VIII of France. Today, even hung with fixed ropes, the climb is still vertical, serious and intimidating if not exactly difficult. In 1492 it was perhaps as fearsome a venture into the unknown as a voyage to the Indies.

With the advent of the Age of Reason and with the justification of scientific research, men started to explore the Alps in a more enlightened frame of mind. Mont Blanc was climbed in 1786 by a local doctor and his guide, the fourth — and first British ascent — being made the following year by a Coldstream Guards Colonel. The Swiss Meyer brothers climbed the Jungfrau in 1811 and the Fionsteraarhorn in 1812.

Alpine historians identify 1854, the year Alfred Wills and his guides climbed the Wetterhorn, as the birthday of Alpinism — of mountaineering per se. The ensuing 11 years — the so-called 'Golden Age of Mountaineering' — saw more than 180 great peaks climbed for the first time. By its close, Alpinism had emerged as a recognisable sport. The guides who climbed with these Golden Age pioneers were local mountain peasants and hunters who developed a proud tradition of comradeship and teamwork with their employers and became a corps d'élite of skilled craftsmen. The skills and ability of both amateur and guide were complementary, a relationship which has long since disappeared. Guideless climbing — the norm today — was not considered respectable until the 1870s.

Mountaineering was at first a purely European activity. The American Alpine Club was established in 1902, an indication perhaps that the west was now won. After the Golden Age many of the Alpine pioneers went on to climb and explore elsewhere; in the Andes and Caucasus for instance, and in 1883 W.W.Graham became the first European to visit the Himalaya just to climb '. . . for sport and adventure . . .'as he put it. Some 90 years were to pass before such visits became commonplace.

At the close of the 20th century the mountains still engender strong emotions, though today they are more typically ones of pleasure and excitement. As we shall see later mountain activities in their various forms have become national sports in Alpine Europe and of serious minority interest elsewhere, especially among the Anglo-Saxon countries and in Japan. But mountains are all things to all men and to the majority of us they represent adventure rather than competition, freedom rather than rules, and new and unlimited horizons. To many others, prevented by circumstances or inclination perhaps from personal involvement in the game, mountains are an inspiration, a source of wonder, indeed the ultimate landscape. Tennyson was no climber but he too was obviously inspired when, from the roof of Milan Cathedral on a clear day , he noted:

> How faintly flush'd, how phantom fair
> Was Monte Rosa, hanging there
> A thousand shadowy pencill'd valleys
> And snowy dells in a golden air.

John Cleare
Fonthill Gifford, Wiltshire, April 1997

# THE EUROPEAN
# ALPS

FAR RIGHT: Vercors,
France. *The extraordinary
limestone mesa of Mont
Aiguille rises only to 6,844ft
(2,086m) but its first ascent
in 1492 by a team led by the
Signeur de Ville is considered
to be the first alpine rock-
climb. The original route is
very steep and exposed and
requires proper climbing
skills, although it is now
equipped with fixed ropes.*

The mountains of the Alps dominate central Europe. Forming a
great chain some 600 miles (965km) long and around 80 miles
(130km) wide, they sweep up from the Mediterranean coast behind
Monaco, curve through the heart of Europe and finally fade away
into the tangled uplands of the Balkans. Here rise Western Europe's
greatest rivers — the Po, the Rhône, the Rhine and those major trib-
utaries of the Danube, the Inn and the Drava. All are born of alpine
snows: indeed one peak in central Switzerland is that geographical
rarity a tri-oceanic watershed, its run-off feeding the North Sea, the
Mediterranean and the Adriatic. Encompassing most of
Switzerland, much of Austria and all of tiny Liechtenstein, standing

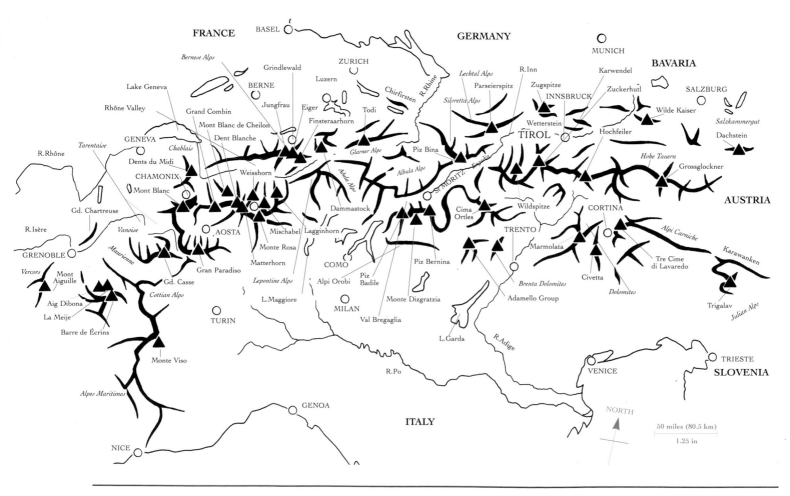

astride the frontiers of no fewer than five other sovereign nations, cradling many of the ancient centres of European civilisation and traversed by time-honoured trade routes between the empires of the Middle Sea and northern Europe, it is not surprising that these are the best known, the best documented and most climbed upon mountains on earth.

Geographically the Alps are composed of dozens of separate sub-ranges, each of different character and appeal, many of their crests defining no-quibble political frontiers. Igneous rocks form many of the central, higher ranges which hold heavy — though currently shrinking — glaciation, while the lower peripheral ranges are typically limestone.

A century and a half ago the sport of mountaineering was born among these mountains and alpinists soon realised that the larger icy peaks are high enough above the valleys to demand serious though not expeditionary commitment, yet not quite high enough to create altitude problems for lowland dwellers. An abundance of alpine refuges, the development of cable cars and other forms of uphill lift and the highly-developed infrastructure of the alpine countries has been such that the Alps are still the crucible of world mountaineering. Here also were invented all the other mountain sports that we know today. Indeed so much have mountains become part of national psyche that alpinism and alpine skiing are acknowledged as major

**South West Alps —
France, Italy**
*Dauphiné, France*
Barre des Écrins (13,455ft/4,101m)
*Vanoise, France*
Grande Casse (12,638ft/3,852m)
*Eastern Graians, Italy*
Gran Paradiso (13,323ft/4,061m)

**Western Alps — Switzerland,
Italy, France**
*Mont Blanc massif, France/Italy/
Switzerland*
Mont Blanc (15,771ft/4,807m),
France
*Pennine Alps, Switzerland/Italy*
Dufourspitze, Monte Rosa
(15,203ft/4,633m), Switzerland
*Bernese Alps, Switzerland*
Finsteraarhorn (14,022ft/4,274m)

**Central Alps — Switzerland,
Italy, Liechtenstein**
Dammastock (11,906ft/3,628m),
Switzerland
*Bernina Alps, Switzerland/Italy*
Piz Bernina (13,284ft/4,049m)
*Bregaglia Alps, Switzerland/Italy*
Monte Dizgratzia (12,067ft/3,678m),
Italy

**Eastern Alps — Austria, Italy,
Germany, Slovenia**
*Ortler Alps, Italy*
Cima Ortles (12,792ft/3,900m)
*Kalkalpen, Austria/Germany*
Parseierspitz (9,961ft/3,036m),
Austria
Zugspitz (9,718ft/2,962m), Germany
*Otztal Alps, Austria/Italy*
Wildspitze (12,375ft/3,772m),
Austria
*Stubai Alps, Austria/Italy*
Zuckerhutl (11,499ft/3,505m)
*Zillertal Alps, Austria/Italy*
Hochfeiler (11,516ft/3,510m),
*Hohe Tauern, Austria*
Gross Glockner (12,461ft/3,798m)
*Dolomites, Italy*
Marmolata (10,965ft/3,342m)
*Julian Alps, Slovenia/Italy*
Trigalev (9,393ft/2,863m), Slovenia

*The tabular sections at the start of each chapter list the highest — not necessarily the most interesting — peaks. The numbers in brackets indicate the highest peaks of the range or the country, whichever is appropriate.*

# THE EUROPEAN
# ALPS

Bernese Alps.
*Panorama from the summit of the Jungfrau. The Pennine Alps stand along the skyline: from left to right, Mont Blanc de Cheilon, Grand Combin, then the Mont Blanc massif with the Grandes Jorasses and Mont Blanc itself prominent. Meanwhile in the foreground below is the head of Lauterbrunnental on the right with, from left to right, the so-called Lauterbrunnen Wall peaks ending with the Lauterbrunnen Breithorn above the two climbers, then the little Tschingelhorn (named after Coolidge's dog), the Tschingelfirn Glacier and the rocky Gspaltenhorn on the right of the glacier.*

# THE EUROPEAN
# ALPS

national sports in each of the five larger alpine countries and internationally through the winter olympics.

Rising from the Mediterranean coast, the southwest Alps run northwards for 150 miles, the Franco-Italian frontier following the watershed crest. Typically the mountains rise sharply from the plains of Piemonte while breaking into a jumble of sub-ranges on the western — French — side where stand the Dauphiné Alps or Massif des Écrins. Savage, craggy and desolate, holding sizeable glaciers and with 23 peaks rising above 12,000ft (3,660m), this is a favourite range for the alpine connoisseur.

The shapely Gran Paradiso, the highest mountain entirely in Italy and an excellent ski ascent, stands further north just before the Alpine chain becomes the western Alps, pivoting as it were on Mont Blanc as it bends abruptly eastward. This magnificent mountain, a giant of almost Himalayan proportions, stands on the frontier, its summit just within France, and is the highest point in Europe west of the Caucasus. It throws down a stupendous 11,000ft (3,400m) southern face into Italy and dominates a compact group of spectacular satellite peaks where avenues of jagged aiguilles line long valley glaciers including the famous seven-mile long Mer de Glace. Two of these peaks, the Grandes Jorrasses and the Petit Dru, each boast one of the six 'Great North Faces' immortalised by the renowned local guide Gaston Rébuffat. Superb red granite and imposing ice-walls provide over 2,000 other guide-booked climbs of all grades and character, while aggressive and competitive climbers from all over the world have made the massif the forcing ground of modern alpinism and arguably the most important single mountain group in the world. The resorts of Chamonix and Courmayeur lie respectively at the French and Italian foot of the mountain — the former, busy, brash and vibrant, is surely the world's foremost mountain resort. The busy Mont Blanc tunnel, a seven-mile (11km) road link completed in 1965, links the motorway networks of France and Italy.

The St Bernard Pass separates the eastern — Swiss — extremity of the massif from the Pennine Alps which stretch 80 miles (130km) along the Swiss/Italian border. Here stand 10 of the 12 highest Alpine giants, typically aloof and alone and noted for long classic climbs on mixed ground; climbs of serious mountaineering interest rather than great technical difficulty. The most notable peaks, such as the incredible Matterhorn, its silhouette the epitome of mountain form and its north face another of the 'Great North Faces', and many-topped Monte Rosa, the highest summit in Switzerland, cluster round the charming if fashionable Swiss village of Zermatt. Olde-worldy, closed to motors and splendidly situated, Zermatt is a far cry in style from Chamonix and must be the most famous mountain resort in the world. For skiers the delightful 'Haute Route' link-

Vanoise, France. *The gorge-like valley of Gliere leads into the heart of the range, the Col de la Vanoise and the popular Félix Faure refuge. A spectacular ski descent leads down the valley to the village of Pralognon. The limestone pinnacle of the Aiguille de la Vanoise (9,173ft/2,796m) rises on the right.*

ing Chamonix to Zermatt and beyond, 60 miles (100km) through the peaks, passes and glaciers of the Pennines, is the most sought-after ski-tour in the world. The Zermatt valley marks the boundary between French and German-speaking Switzerland.

The Bernese Alps, a knot of formidable ice-hung peaks rising above a tangle of great glaciers, parallel the Pennines northward across the deep, fertile upper valley of the Rhône. Here 37 summits rise above 12,000ft (3,660m) while the 15-mile (25km) Aletsch glacier is the longest in the Alps. Best known of these mountains are the Jungfrau, the Mönch and the frowning Eiger whose notorious *Nordwand* (north face) is the most formidable of the 'Great North Faces'. These peaks are part of the 'Oberland', the northern wall of the range overlooking the smart resort of Grindlewald with the plains of northwest Europe beyond. Despite fickle weather and often poor rock, the Bernese Alps are known for classic mixed routes and the largest concentration of great ice climbs in the Alps.

Embracing the headwaters of both the Rhône and the Rhine, the mountains of eastern Switzerland are defined as the Central Alps. Typically the peaks here are smaller and less renowned, though there are several notable exceptions, and the region is known more for its winter ski tours than its notable climbs. However in the far southeastern corner of Switzerland, ranged along the Italian frontier, stand the compact Bernina and Bregaglia groups. This is Romansch-speaking territory and several of the tiny and exquisite border villages are as fine as any in the Alps, though suave St Moritz, the local centre, is the ultra-fashionable resort of princes. Piz Bernina, the most easterly 13,000ft (4,000m) mountain in the Alps, is highest of a small group of attractive and entirely ice-hung peaks surrounded by quite large glaciers which drain into the Engadin valley to become the River Inn. The adjoining Bregaglia is a chain of sharp granite peaks well known for superb rock-climbs ranking with the best in the Alps. Chief among them is the sweeping 3,000ft (915m) northeast face of the imposing Piz Badile, another of the celebrated 'Great North Faces', but the summits here are comparatively low and recent glacier retreat is tragically jeopardising the several notable ice climbs in the area.

Filling most of Austria, much of northeastern Italy and extending just into Slovenia, the eastern Alps cover the final 250 miles (400km) of mountains. Here the main alpine crest rises to several icy and quite high massifs before fading away towards the gates of Vienna. The main groups are the Ötztal, Stubai and spiky Zillertal massifs astride the frontier separating Austrian North Tyrol from Italian South Tyrol, and the extensive and heavily glaciated Hohe Tauern range entirely in Austria. Here stands the magnificent Grossglockner, Austria's highest peak, and some 50 other summits

Dauphiné Alps, France. *The sharp granite spire of the Aiguille Dibona (10,270ft/3,130m) is perhaps the most spectacular peak in France and several first class rock climbs lead up its southern flank to its tiny summit. Ian Howell is seen on the summit preparing to rope down the short but exposed north arête, the regular descent route.*

ABOVE: Mont Blanc massif, France. *The Aiguille de Bionnassay (13,294ft/4,000m), though one of Mont Blanc's closer satellites, is a fine peak in its own right. It is seen here from the northeast on the slopes of the Dôme du Goûter during a descent from Mont Blanc towards the Goûter hut.*

RIGHT: Mont Blanc massif, France. *The Aiguille du Dru (12,316ft/3,754m) is seen from Montenvers at sunrise. The many-pinnacled ridge on the right of the summit is known as the Arête de Flammes de Pierre. The guide book describes the Dru as possibly the most famous granite pyramid in the world — it is certainly well seen from the popular mountain railway station at Montenvers.*

FAR RIGHT: Mont Blanc massif, France. *Alpenrose (R. ferrugineum) provides a colourful foreground to this view over the Arve valley to the Mer de Glace with the north face of the Grandes Jorasses in the distance at its head. The Aiguilles des Grandes Charmoz with its subsidiary Aiguille de la République is seen on the right while the Montenvers hotel and railway terminus can be discerned above the glacier snout.*

Mont Blanc massif, France. *Dawn behind the Dent du Géant — view from southwest near the Col de Rochefort. This distinctive fang rises to 13,166ft/4,013m on the Franco-Italian frontier ridge and is a conspicuous feature throughout the Mer de Glace basin.*

# THE EUROPEAN ALPS

above 10,000ft (3,000m). However the very highest summits in the Eastern Alps rise in the compact, icy and almost isolated Ortler massif, virtually a spur of the Bernina jutting deep into Italy.

Northwards, beyond the deep valley of the Inn and more or less astride the Bavarian frontier, the succession of Northern Limestone Ranges or Kalkalpen parallels the main chain. These small, wild and craggy rock peaks are snow-free in summer and ever popular with walkers and climbers. Among the several groups is the Wetterstein where the Zugspitz is Germany's highest summit, and the Karwendal, at whose foot lies lovely Innsbruck, the ancient capital of the Tirol. The Wilde Kaiser and Dachstein massifs are especially renowned for their rock climbs.

South of the main chain, the Dolomites are a confusion of dramatic limestone spires and impossible-looking yellow walls extending across 80 miles (130km) of northern Italy. With a centre at the Winter Olympic resort of Cortina, this beautiful region is a paradise for high standard rock climbers and mountain walkers. Climbing routes are invariably steep and frequently overhanging and those on the 2,000ft (600m) south face of the Marmolata — the highest peak — and on the impending north faces of the Cima Ovest and Cima Grande di Lavaredo are of world repute, the latter being the sixth and last of the 'Great North Faces'.

Eastwards and just into the new republic of Slovenia the wild and beautiful Julian Alps form a final knot of mountains. Trigalev, with its excellent limestone climbs is the culminating point. As varied as any range on earth, the European Alps offer almost anything the mountain lover could desire.

RIGHT: Mont Blanc massif, France. *Alpenglow on the Dôme du Goûter (14,121ft/4,304m) Evening view from the Goûter Refuge, the climbing hut used by one of the two regular ascent routes on Mont Blanc.*

BELOW: Pennine Alps. *Dawn is a very special time for all alpinists who must necessarily start their climbs well before first light. This is a dawn view from about 11,500ft (3,500m) up on the Pigne d'Arolla northeastwards towards the distant peaks of the Bernese Alps beyond the Rhône Valley.*

# A Date with Dizgratzia

THERE was time for just one more climb. The season was over; my mate had gone home and I was on my own at Maloja for a couple of days. Monte Dizgratzia beckoned. A sharp and shapely snow peak, the highest summit in the Bergell, it rises just in Italy on a spur off the main ridge. I'd seen it from afar and had once even tried to climb it before getting lost in poor weather among the jumble of hanging glaciers and sub-peaks on the Italian flank. It was unfinished business. I'd try it solo.

In the late afternoon I hiked up the long dusty glen to the Forno Hut — a friendly place run by the cheery Yorkshire wife of Hans Phillp, a young and accomplished local guide. I was sure of a welcome. There were pleasant associations too, for it was from here that I had one night watched the moon hanging full over the black crest of Castello as the hut radio relayed live the first lunar landing. I was surprised that I'd taken only two hours to complete the seven-mile (11km) slog up from Maloja, halving my time of a week before.

Hans expressed no surprise at my plans beyond suggesting that I'd probably need to overnight in the Mello bivvy hut, strategically sited on the long rocky ridge linking Dizgratzia to the main Bergell. I left the sleeping hut at 3.30am into the silent night.

Moving steadily uphill before dawn is a bittersweet experience. Your body is hot but the sweat on your back beneath the rucksack is cold and clammy. Your stubbled face is raw and your lips are dry in the crisp air. Only your eyes watch the dawn arrive for your mind is slow until it thaws in the cosy glare of the new sun. Three miles (5km) and 3,000ft (915m) of easy but crevasse-strewn snowfields took me through the dawn to the frontier ridge at the summit of Monte Sissone. I plotted the the landmarks on my route, thrown into sharp relief by the early sunshine, before scrambling down the broken southern crags onto steep névé down which I glissaded towards the misty blue abyss of the Val di Mello. Somewhere down here was the Roma Traverse — a high-level path connecting the huts in the southern Italian cwms of the Bergell via a succession of passes in the jagged intervening ridges. Finding it should guarantee finding the passes but, anxious not to lose more height than necessary, I must have kept too high. Instead I clambered across awkward broken slopes but at least in the right direction.

Eventually I found myself below a rock needle I had seen from Sissone, a miniature of the famous Grand Capucin: ahead were steep glacier slopes upwards to a rocky crest. Somewhere up there was the Passo Cecilia, a secret passage in the ridges like the staggered entrance to an Iron Age hill fort. Leading onto the Preda Rossa Glacier, it was the key to the southwestern cirque of Dizgratzia itself.

On with crampons and a rhythmic 1,600ft (500m) climb found the Passo without difficulty. For the first time since dawn I allowed my mind to wander. Contrary to what people might imagine, the excitement of solo climbing is subconscious. Moving fast over difficult and hazardous terrain demands great concentration, and despite the delight in being entirely self-sufficient, a delight akin to fear perhaps, the business of safe navigation allows no time for idle musing. The mind is totally occupied with the task in hand. On this long methodical plod however, where the only break was the occasional crevasse that required negotiating or the quick about-turn from leftward zig to rightward zag, I could consciously enjoy for the first time my loneness and the challenge I had set myself.

The snow on the Preda Rossa glacier was already softening as I joined a well-trodden line of footsteps leading up to the lowest point in the ridge forming the head of the cirque — the northwest ridge of Dizgratzia itself. This must be the route from the Ponti Hut — the regular route. I could see a couple of parties high on the ridge, slow moving dots against the cobalt emptiness of the sky. I overtook a labouring rope of three with a cheery 'Buon giorno', climbed over a couple of awkward schrunds and arrived on the ridge. In a light breeze I slipped on my windproof. And now only 1,000ft (300m) to the summit.

Dizgratzia was first climbed in August 1862 by a renowned party: Leslie Stephen, Edward Kennedy and Thomas Cox with their guide Melchior Anderegg had ascended this very ridge. A narrow rock crest alternated with an ice arête to give easy but extremely exposed climbing that demanded continuous concentration. Occasionally I paused to allow descending ropes to pass or to peer over the edge at the intimidating north face. I recognised the steep Spigolo Inglese, the ice rib climbed in 1910 by the great Scots pioneers, Raeburn and Ling — the first route on the face and said not to be easy. Then I was above the central part of the face where a hanging icefield swept down below a summit rock-band towards the top of the great pillar. Below that only the dappled depths of the Val Sissone.

The summit was a rocky plinth but to reach it I had to make an exposed and awkward bridging move over the top of an icy chimney. It was 10.45am; I ate a little food and took some photographs. In a zinc container below the metal cross was the summit book and I was able to find only two other Anglo-Saxon entries over the past dozen years. One was Eric Shipton, the other an American climber I knew. But afternoon snow is dangerous so I was soon retracing my steps, down, down, carefully downwards until this time I found the elusive Roma Traverse.

I was back at the Forno Hut just after 4.0 where a much surprised Hans plied me with tea. Then I trotted down in the dusk to Maloja, my tent and gallons more tea. And the next year I came back and climbed the north face but that is another story..

Bernese Alps. *The setting sun casts an eerie Brocken Spectre in the mist that clings to the summit crest of the Eiger (13,025ft/3,970m) where a small camp has been established between the snow cornice and the top of the steep rocky south face.*

# THE EUROPEAN
# ALPS

ABOVE: Pennine Alps.
*Two ski-mountaineers ascend the steep Tsena Réfien glacier in new snow after a spring storm en route to the Col de Serpentine and the Pigne d'Arolla summit. This is an alternative stage on the famous Haute Route. Beyond rises the northern flank of the beautiful Mont Blanc de Cheilon (12,696ft/3,870m).*

RIGHT: Bernese Alps.
*The classic Mittellegi or northeast ridge of the Eiger (13,025ft/3,970m).*

Pennine Alps. *Strange lenticular clouds float over the the incredible Matterhorn (14,690ft/4,478m) in this dawn view westwards from Monte Rosa hut.*

# Entertainment at Chamonix

THE north face of the Aiguille du Midi, a 4,000ft (1,200m) pyramid of rock and ice, dominates Chamonix. The famous Midi téléferique (cable car), highest in the Alps, sweeps up from the town in two bounds: the first a mere 4,000ft (1,200m) to Plan de l'Aiguille, a grassy alp above the forest, the second a dizzy 5,000ft (1,500m) to the needle-like summit of the aiguille itself. While definitely environmentally incorrect, the cable car is impressive engineering and makes possible serious climbs in a single day out from the valley fleshpots.

One day we decided to look at the Éperon Central — the central spur on this very face. Climbed only once before, and that in two days by a famous French guide who'd said it was quite hard, it promised to provide good sport. But we were well back in the dawn queue for the cable car and it was well after 7.00am that we eventually disembarked at Plan de l'Aiguille and set off up meadow, moraine and steepening glacier towards the bottom of the face a mile distant.

The initial rocks were not steep and on the first little wall we were able to swing up on a rusty wire cable, obviously discarded during the téléferique construction. 'If ye want the rope give a shout,' cried Tom as he forged ahead. 'Ah think weel no want it fur a while but ahm no happy aboot the weather!'

Rusty, Chris and I scrambled breathlessly onwards up steps and rocky ribs linked by snow patches but Tom was always ahead, leading round, behind or over each obstacle. He had an eye for a line, a genius which turned every problem into a feasible route upwards.

We caught up with him below a steep dièdre where he was uncoiling his rope. 'Lewks harrd — belay me,' he muttered and he was off again, bridging wide on the rough granite. The pitch was not easy and above it we paused on the snowy ledge to rest, eat and take stock. We'd been climbing for only four hours and already we were half way up. Great! but there had to be harder climbing ahead. Only then was I conscious of the téléferique cable, seemingly only a stone's throw out into space. Every few minutes a cabin swooped silently past on the now almost vertical cable, windows crammed with tourists eager to glimpse 'les vrai alpinists'. But the

Bernese Alps. *The Eiger rises over Kleine Scheidegg. The famous Nordwand, most formidable of the six 'Great North Faces', is on the left with the regular route, the east flank, on the right. It is early autumn and the snow cover is abnormally light especially on the north face itself, where the hanging ice fields are hardly visible.*

weather looked threatening; below us the cable cars plunged into a layer of grey cloud that obscured the valley and it was suddenly cold.

Roped up now, Tom with Chris and Rusty with me, we cramponed up a steep ice couloir and entered a maze of short steep walls and icy grooves. Mist and snowflakes swirled around us. Once I had to remove my gloves to use some small holds and I recall weeping in agony as they regained feeling once more. Conditions became decidedly awkward and we all moved very carefully, belaying now on every pitch. The earlier exhilaration of swift movement on warm rock had degenerated into a slow painful clawing upwards. Thunder rolled ominously over towards Mont Blanc and my back was wet with cold sweat.

Suddenly, still some way ahead and above an evil-looking wall of ice-plastered rock, the téléferique station appeared through a rent in the mist. No way! So near and yet so far. The vision faded into driving snow and we moved out leftwards into a white world of seracs and ice fields which could only be the final slopes. Here we could

move together again and get warm. Tom consulted his watch when we paused for breath. 'Last télé's in half an 'oor,' he exclaimed. 'Ah'm buggered if ah'm bivouacking. Ah'l poosh on an' hold the last car for ye!' And he was gone, cramponing off into the enveloping whiteness at a steady lope.

Agonisingly slowly the three of us wound our way through the ice walls and round the crevasses and then the angle eased. We heard a humming noise, a black hole gaped in the snow bank ahead, and a line of lights led into the mountain. 'Off with yer crampons,' shouted Chris, 'Run, run!' And we went pounding down the echoing corridors into the warm smell of tourists and machinery.

'Vite! Vite!' cried a muffled figure in blue uniform and there was Tom beside the cable car door, snow plastered in his hair and a wide grin on his face. 'Ah just made it, told them ye could'na bivouac withoot me!' And then we were swooping downwards through the grey murk and the gathering darkness.

# THE EUROPEAN
# ALPS

Bernese Alps.
*Climbers approach the
Rottalsattel en route to the
Jungfrau summit by the
south ridge. Beyond is the
pyramid of the Mönch with
the Eiger visible behind it.
The Jungfraujoch is the wide
saddle on the left while the
Obermönchjoch is the col to
the right of the Mönch.*

Bernese Alps.
*Alpenglow and moonrise over
the Schreckhorn (left —
13,379ft/4,078m) and
Lauteraarhorn (right).
The Wetterhorn is seen in
distance on the left. View
from the Obermönchjoch.*

# EUROPE

**Caucasus — Russian Federation, Georgia, Azerbaijan**
*(1) Elbrus (18,481ft/5,633m)*
*(2) Dykh-Tau (17,074ft/5,204m)*
*(3) Shkhara (17,064ft/5,201m)*
*Ushba South (15,453ft/4,701m)*
*Shkhelda (14,173ft/4,320m)*

Mountaineering — as a recreational activity in its own right — was born in Europe and even today Europe's premier mountains, the Alps, are considered the crucible of the sport. All the mountain activities we now enjoy were nurtured to maturity by

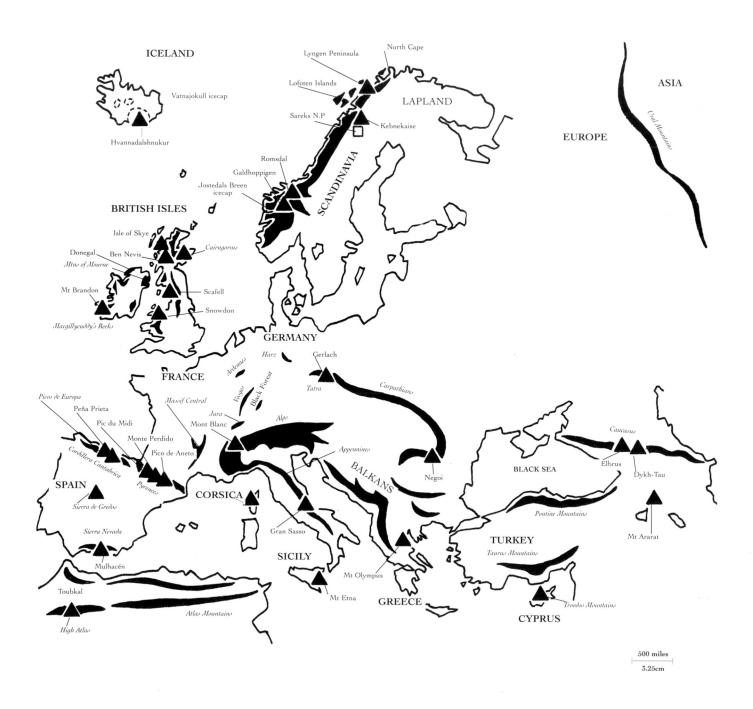

ICELAND

Vatnajokull icecap

Hvannadalshnukur

North Cape

Lyngen Peninsula

Lofoten Islands

LAPLAND

Sareks N.P

Kebnekaise

ASIA

EUROPE

*Ural Mountains*

Romsdal

Galdhoppigen

Jostedals Breen icecap

SCANDINAVIA

BRITISH ISLES

Isle of Skye

*Cairngorms*

Donegal    Ben Nevis

*Mtns of Mourne*

Mt Brandon    Scafell

Snowdon

*Macgillycuddy's Reeks*

GERMANY

*Harz*

Gerlach

*Ardennes*

*Vosges*    *Black Forest*

*Carpathians*

Tatra

FRANCE

Picos de Europa

Peña Prieta

Pic du Midi

Monte Perdido

*Massif Central*

*Jura*

*Alps*

Mont Blanc

Pico de Aneto

*Cordillera Cantabrica*

*Pyrenees*

SPAIN

*Sierra de Gredos*

*Appennines*

BALKANS

Negoi

*Caucasus*

BLACK SEA

Elbrus

Dykh-Tau

CORSICA

*Sierra Nevada*

Gran Sasso

SICILY

*Pontine Mountains*

TURKEY

Mt Ararat

Mulhacén

*Taurus Mountains*

Mt Olympus

Toubkal

Mt Etna

GREECE

*Troodos Mountains*

*Atlas Mountains*

CYPRUS

*High Atlas*

500 miles

3.25cm

European exponents — not always alpine natives but those able to practise and refine their crafts among their own home mountains.

Isolating Spain from the rest of Europe, the Pyrenees form a single narrow chain some 270 miles (435km) from sea to sea. While more than 50 peaks rise above 10,000ft (3,000m), only three top 11,000ft (3,350m) while snow patches linger through the summer and small glaciers still cling to the northern flanks of the higher summits. The area is typically either granite or limestone, the latter forming the characteristic cliff-girt cirques, such as that at Gavarnie, for which the range is renowned. The regular ascent of any Pyrenean summit is rarely more than a scramble but there is fine rock climbing in the area and peaks such as the Vignemale and Pic du Midi d'Ossau are known for some formidable routes. There are several ski resorts besides challenging ski-touring and strenuous walking throughout the range. Though there are mountain huts in popular areas, much of the Pyrenees is still wild and comparatively undeveloped.

Spain's highest summits rise close to Grenada within sight of the Mediterranean. The Sierra Nevada are gentle peaks, snowless in summer but with popular winter skiing. There is good rock climbing in the Gredos Range of central Spain but the finest mountains stand in the far north. The Picos de Europa behind the port of Santander are the culminating knot of the lengthy Cordillera Cantabrica that parallels the Biscay coast and their arid wilderness, limestone spires and lush valleys echo the Dolomites and offer rugged scrambling and hiking besides excellent rock climbing. The monolithic tower of Naranjo de Bulnes, up which the easiest route is a serious rock climb, is the most famous mountain in Spain. Good hiking and ski-touring are found among the shapely but less craggy mountains elsewhere in the Cantabrica.

Other notable ranges of southern Europe are the Italian Apennines and the extremely rugged mountains of Corsica, a charming island which possesses a 35-mile (56km) crest of fine granite peaks the traverse of which is a renowned if gruelling multi-day expedition. There is also much good rock climbing and some interesting ski-touring. By contrast the Apennines extend over 700 miles (1,100km) to form the entire spine of Italy, encompassing many very diverse mountain areas. There are smooth, shapely summits, craggy hillsides and forested plateaux. There is climbing on rock and ice, fine hiking and many small ski resorts. Most spectacular are the limestone massifs of the Abruzzo region northeast of Rome where Corno Grande is the loftiest summit of the popular 20-mile (32km) long Gran Sasso massif, the highest of the Apennines. Here tiny Calderone, Europe's most southerly glacier, lies among the imposing limestone towers.

### Apennines — Italy
(1) *Gran Sasso/Corno Grande* (9,554ft/2,912m)
(2) *Monte della Maiella/Monte Amaro* (9,170ft/2,795m)
*Monte Velino* (8,156ft/2,486m)
*Monte Sibillini/Monte Vettore* (8,123ft/2,476m)

### Corsica — France
(1) *Monte Cinto* (8,878/2,706m)
*Monte Rotondo* (8,602ft/2,622m)

### Pyrenees — France, Spain, Andorra
(1) *Pico de Aneto* (11,168ft/3,404m)
(2) *Pico de Posets* (11,073ft/3,375m)
(3) *Monte Perdido* (11,007ft/3,355m)
*Vignemale* (10,820ft/3,298)

### Spain
*Sierra Nevada*
(1) *Mulhacén* (11,421ft/3,481m)

*Sierra de Gredos*
(1) *Pico de Almanzor* (8,504ft/2,592m)

*Picos de Europa*
(1) *Torre Cerredo* (8,688ft/2,648m)
*Naranjo de Bulnes* (8,264ft/2,519m)

*Cordillera Cantabrica*
*Peña Prieta* (8,446ft/2,575m)

### Scandinavia
*Jotunheimen, Norway*
(1) *Galdhøpiggen* (8,098ft/2,468m)
(2) *Glittertind* (8,045ft/2,452m)
(3) *Skagastølstind* (7,888ft/2,404m)

*Lyngen, Norway*
(1) *Jiekkevarre* (6,053ft/1,845m), Norway

*Romsdale, Norway*
(1) *Trolltind* (5,888ft/1,795m)

*Torne Lappmark, Sweden*
(1) *Kebnekaise* (6,926ft/2,111m)

### British Isles
*Scotland*
(1) *Ben Nevis* (4,406ft/1,343m)
(5) *Cairngorm* (4,084ft/1,245m)
*Wales*
(1) *Snowdon — yr Wyddfa* (3,560ft/1,085m)
*Ireland*
(1) *Carrauntoohil* (3,414ft/1,0421m)
*England*
(1) *Scafell Pike* (3,210ft/978m)

# EUROPE

Picos de Europa, Spain. *Peaks of the Andara or eastern massif rise over the little village of Hojedo near the local centre of Potes. It is early May and the mountains are still snow-covered while spring has already sprung in the lush Dava Valley.*

Stretching 550 miles (885km) between the Black and Caspian Seas, the Caucasus is Europe's border with Asia Minor. Comparable to the Alps in style and scenery if rather higher and rather less extensive, the range offers some of the best mountaineering in the world. Most interesting is the central section where a series of formidable rock and ice peaks cluster round several savage glacier cirques. Among notable summits are Shkhara whose 6,000ft (1,830m) north face rises from the Bezingi Basin, most famous of these cirques, and twin-fanged Ushba, the Matterhorn of the Caucasus. Elbruz, by far Europe's highest summit, is rather out of character. Standing north off the main crest, its gentle glaciers cloak an extinct volcanic cone and give a straightforward approach on foot or ski to its twin summits.

The Carpathians are the all-but ubiquitous range of eastern Europe. Rising gently near Vienna, forming the borders of the Czech Republic, Slovakia, Poland, most of Hungary, and traversing the Ukraine and Romania, these highlands define the northern Danube watershed. Only in two places do their forested hills rise high: Negoi, 70 miles (110km) from Bucharest, is the summit of wild Transylvania where gothic legend locates the home of Dracula; the other lies astride the Slovakian/Polish frontier south of Krakow. This latter region is the Tatra, three small mountain groups of disparate character, of which the central, the High Tatra, is a compact chain of spectacular bare granite peaks with steep crags, jagged ridges and deep corries which often cradle beautiful tarns. Blanketed by heavy snow in winter, the World Ski Championships have twice been held at Zakopane, the bustling little resort on the Polish side. Needless to say there is good scrambling to many of the summits, superb rock and ice climbing and a well-maintained network of popular hiking trails.

Europe's most extensive mountain system is the complex tangle of ranges that runs the 1,000-mile (1,600km) length of Norway, a rugged country that is 70 percent mountainous. Almost 300 summits rise above 6,000ft (1,800m), many sheer from the fjord-indented coastline. Several vestigial icecaps include the largest in Europe, the Jostedals Breen, and there are dozens of small glaciers, yet the proximity of the warm Gulf Stream ensures a milder climate than the latitude might suggest, even among that third of the mountains that lie beyond the Arctic Circle. While hardly alpine in character, Norwegian mountains abound with steep rock, frequently taking the form of sharp granite peaks such as chisel-shaped Store Skagastølstind or incredible gneiss cliffs like Romsdal's famous Troll Wall, plumb vertical for over 4,000ft (1,200m). Notable among the ranges of the far north are the spikey gabbro peaks of the Lofoten Islands sweeping up from the sea and the shapely snow-capped

summits of the lovely Lyngen Peninsula just east of Tromsø. Over
the frontier into Sweden the higher mountains rise from a desolate,
more arctic landscape. Kebnekaise is of little climbing interest but
the knot of mountains some 50 miles (80km) southward in the
Sareks National Park can claim more attention.

Though insignificant in terms of size, the mountains of the British
Isles have exerted a tremendous influence on world mountaineering.
That apart, the climate, the geography, the ever varying geology and
the fact that these uplands were all once heavily glaciated and rise
never far from the sea, render them exceptionally beautiful and as
worthy as any. The altitude yard-stick by which British and Irish
mountains are usually gauged is 3,000ft (915m) although frequently peaks of lesser height are of greater interest. All four of England's
3,000-footers stand in the popular and picturesque Lake District
where rocky-topped Scafell Pike is easily ascended. More dramatic
if slightly lower is neighbouring Scafell itself, a fine mountain whose
great northern crags hold many famous climbs. In all there are 108

Picos de Europa, Spain.
*The Garganta del Cares
gorge divides the western
from the central massif of
the Picos. These limestone
walls and pinnacles rise
above the gorge near the tiny
mountain village of Bulnes.*

# EUROPE

fells topping 2,000ft (600m) in the Lake District. Most of Wales is mountainous but the Snowdonia region of North Wales can boast 15 tops above 3,000ft (915m) and typically they are sharper, steeper and more rugged than the English mountains. Snowdon itself — Yr Wyddfa — is a craggy pyramid unfortunately defiled by a victorian steam-driven rack-railway, though its summit can also be reached by the excitingly narrow rock arête of the Snowdon Horseshoe. Triple-topped Tryfan is the only summit outside Scotland, whose route of easiest ascent demands the use of hands.

The Scottish Highlands are Western Europe's greatest wilderness area, occupying one fifth of the land area of the United Kingdom. Here rise seven 4,000ft (1,200m) summits and over 500 tops above the magic 3,000ft (915m) level. Text book examples of post-glacial scenery abound, corrie and crag, moraine and erratic, fjord and tarn. There are sharp mountains, craggy mountains and rounded mountains. Winter snow is heavy and the higher summits enjoy an arctic-alpine climate. This is especially true of Ben Nevis, rising straight from a lengthy sea-loch and holding small patches of permanent snow on its huge northeast precipices, and of the high Cairngorm plateau in whose deep corries some of the best Scottish skiing is found. The magnificence of the jagged Cuillin mountains on the Isle of Skye is legendary.

Ireland is surprisingly mountainous and the island is ringed by small if intriguing mountains. Although the two eastern 3,000-footers (915m) are little more than large hills, Carrauntoohil and the other nine tops of Macgillycuddy's Reeks in Co. Kerry are linked by craggy ridges above a series of fine corries. Isolated, mist-wreathed, deep-sculpted Mount Brandon on Kerry's Dingle Peninsula is notable as the most westerly mountain in Europe. It said that on a clear day the American coast can be seen from its summit.

Pyrenees, Spain. *Ian Howell prepares the evening brew at a bivouac some 8,500ft (c2,600m) up on the hillside of El Fraile below Monte Perdido on the Spanish side of the frontier in the Ordesa National Park. This is ideal country for hardy hill-walkers travelling light.*

Pyrenees, Spain/France.
*The Franco-Spanish frontier
crest is seen to the southwest
over the head of the deep
Gavarnie Valley from the
Hourquette (pass) d'Alans.
The peculiar deep gash of
the famous Brèche Roland
is well seen.*

# EUROPE

Cordillera Cantabrica, Spain. *Peña Prieta (8,448ft/2,575m) is the highest summit in the range outside the Picos massif. In this early May view a ski-mountaineer scrambles along the narrow ridge from the summit towards the western top. The gentle summit on the right is the Mojon de las Tres Provincias.*

# A Night on Ben Nevis

IT was dawn on New Year's Eve. To reach the Buachaille Etive Mor, the mountain on which we intended to climb, we must first cross the frozen Coupal, a mountain river no more than waist deep close by the bothy at Jacksonville but all of 20 yards (18m) wide. I went first and the ice broke under me. The water was very cold and I was very wet. It was no way to start a serious winter climb in Glencoe. By the time we had retired to our camp, had a hot brew and donned dry clothes the short winter day was well advanced. So just for the hell of it we decided we would climb Ben Nevis and see in the New Year from a bivouac on its summit. Tony and I were both young and, at the time, it seemed an exciting thing to do.

In Glen Nevis the frost was still white on the little meadows for in winter no sun reaches its narrow floor. But the bare alders beside the river rose stark against a blue sky and before we reached the snow line we were enjoying that crisp glowing low-angled sunshine that is so special about the Highland winter. The Ben was well plastered with snow but the weather had been good for several days and the going on the long ascent was no problem. We even had to crampon up the steep slopes beside the Red Burn. We found the snow on the wide summit plateau ribbed with miniature sastrugi, the only features the deeply drifted ruins of the old observatory and the white mound of the nearby summit cairn. We knew that huge cornices edge the plateau lip overhanging the 1,800ft (600m) crags of the northeast face so we kept well clear of the edge and made for the Observatory. Dusk was already on us as we scooped out a hollow in the lee of one of the tumbled walls, and in it erected our flimsy tent.

Well prepared, we knew how to make ourselves comfortable and donning most of our spare clothing we burrowed into our sleeping bags. I can't recall exactly what sort of meal we cooked on our small primus but it can only have been rudimentary, before we got down to the more serious business of brewing hot drinks. These I

Central Highlands, Scotland. *Two hill-walkers are approaching the summit of Carn Mor Dearg (4,012ft/1,223m) in mid-June. Seen beyond to the right is the huge northwest face of Ben Nevis, the highest section of Britain's highest mountain. The Ben's summit itself is on the plateau edge just to the left of the large snow-filled gully — Tower Gully. The famous Northeast Buttress is the black, steeply-falling, left-hand skyline.*

# EUROPE

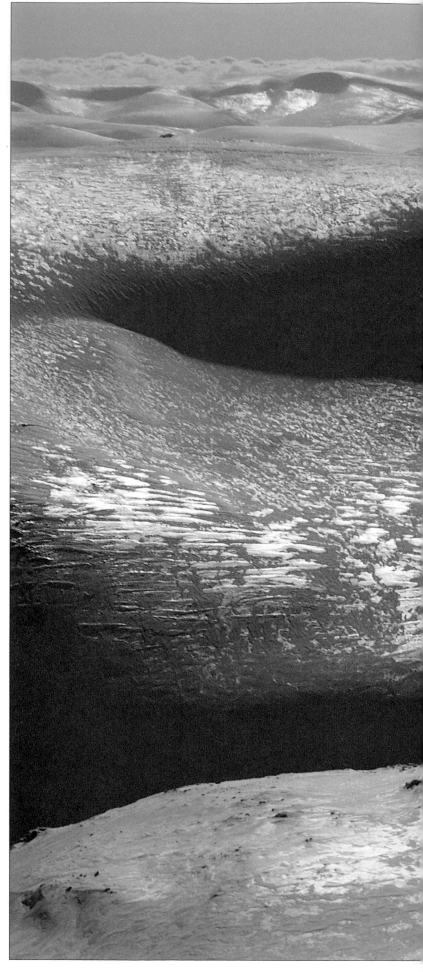

remember as a continuous sequence of steaming mugs of hot sweet lemon tea liberally laced with scotch. Such diversions take time and that night we had plenty of that. But as midnight approached we remembered the purpose of our little expedition and almost reluctantly we retrieved our boots from our sleeping bags, struggled into windproofs, gloves and balaclavas, and crawled out into the night.

The frost held all Scotland in its grip. Across the plateau the moon was near full and it hung low over Loch Linnhe shimmering a silver pathway to the islands of Mull, Colonsay and distant Islay, black shapes against the sea. Westwards were the crystal teeth of the Skye and Rhum Cuillin hanging above the shadowed cornices and black void of Tower Gully. And floating beyond, neither sea nor sky, a hint that was perhaps the Outer Isles? Or Tir-na-Og maybe?

Northwards, white in the moonlight, mountain rose beyond mountain, crest beyond crest into a far distance behind which the massed artillery of the Aurora thundered out in eerie silence. Half the sky blazed with its flames, great flashes of blue and red and green stabbing into the black dome above us. But the only sound was the creaking of the snow beneath our boots, the pulsing of the stars and our beating hearts. I had not seen the Lights before. It was a night to remember.

In those days it was our habit to climb in Scotland for a few days every New Year and we had so enjoyed our night on the Ben — the almost mystic experience had really set us up for the ensuing 12 months — that we thought to repeat the exercise. Aware that we had been lucky to enjoy perfect weather, this year we equipped ourselves with a decent mountain tent and top quality survival gear. Unfortunately, but as is more usual of course, the New Year was blasted in on the wings of a blizzard. We battled through 16 hours of darkness to prevent the tent from collapsing under the weight of driven snow. It was just another of those squalid nights that is an adventure only in retrospect.

Cairngorms, Scotland.
*This winter view of the eastern Highlands looks southward from the summit of Cairngorm itself (4,084ft/1,245m), over the deep trough holding remote Loch Avon, towards the shadowed pyramid of Beinn Mheadhoin (3,883ft/1,184m) and the sea of summits beyond, illustrating the arctic-alpine environment of the higher Scottish tops, an ancient plateau carved out by glaciers.*

# EUROPE

Pyrenees, France. *View eastwards from the Col des Sarradets towards Pic du Marbore (10,656ft/3,248m) rising over the head of the Gavarnie Cirque. The Refuge des Sarradets (climbing hut at 8,488ft/2,587m) can be seen in mid-distance on the right.*

Pyrenees, France. *The famous Vignemalle massif is seen in the far distance just right of centre in this view westward over the Gavarnie valley from the Hourquette d'Alans. This French flank of the range provides a contrast to the more arid southern, Spanish, side of the watershed.*

Lyngen Peninsula, Arctic Norway. *Peaks of the Stora Lenangestinde massif rise over 5,200ft (1,590m). Tundra, bog and forests of dwarf birch stretch up to the summer in this view from the northwest near the settlement of Kobbenes.*

Arctic Norway. *The peak of Vaggastindan (4,587ft/ 1,398m) overlooks fishing boats at anchor in the Nordlenangen Fjord near the tip of the Lyngen Peninsula: a midsummer view.*

# EUROPE

Arctic Norway. *The saw-tooth mountains of the island of Kvalöy (Store Blåmennen — 3,425ft/1,044m) dominate the western horizon in this midnight view at mid-summer from the heights of Storsteinnen above the world's northernmost city: Tromso, itself seen at the bottom of the picture on the shores of the fjord.*

Arctic Norway. *The myriad craggy islands off the Norwegian coasts hold many small but beautiful mountains. In this April picture a fishing boat is leaving the little settlement of Bergsfjord on the island of Loppa off the Finnmark coast not far from the North Cape. The mountains seen in the picture rise over 2,700ft (824m) and there are three small permanent icecaps on the island.*

Snowdonia, North Wales. *Yr Wyddfa, Snowdon's summit, is seen from the neighbouring peak of Crib-y-Ddysgl, one of the summits of the famous Snowdon Horseshoe ridge.*

Lake District, England. *View eastwards from Yewbarrow mountain over the green meadows of Wasdale Head, one of the more remote Lakeland valleys, towards the Scafell massif. Scafell Pike (3,210ft/978m), the highest point in England, stands on the left of the coombe of Hollow Stones; craggier Scafell, just 48ft (14.5m) lower, rises on the right.*

# THE HIMALAYA

In Asia, at approximately 75°east 37°north, there is a hypothetical point known as the Pamir Knot. A dozen titanic folds radiate from here like spokes of a wheel to form the great mountain ranges of Central Asia. The Himalaya is but the longest and the highest of these ranges, a crystal wall separating the teeming plains, the lush valleys and the ancient cultures of India, Nepal and Bhutan from the arid and empty plateaux of the world's roof — from Tibet and China. Not surprisingly, the Himalaya are sacred to both Hindu and Buddhist.

Three mighty rivers entirely contain this mighty range: the Tsangpo or Brahmaputra, the Ganges and the Indus, each draining to the Indian Ocean. The limits of the Himalaya are thus well defined for the Tsangpo carves a horseshoe gorge round the foot of Namche Barwa, the far eastern bastion of the range, only to be emulated in the far west where the Indus loops around the base of Nanga Parbat. These two peaks are separated by 1,400 miles (2,250km) of the most varied mountain scenery on earth.

The Assam and Bhutan Himalaya of the far southeast, strongly influenced by the monsoon and consequently lush and heavily

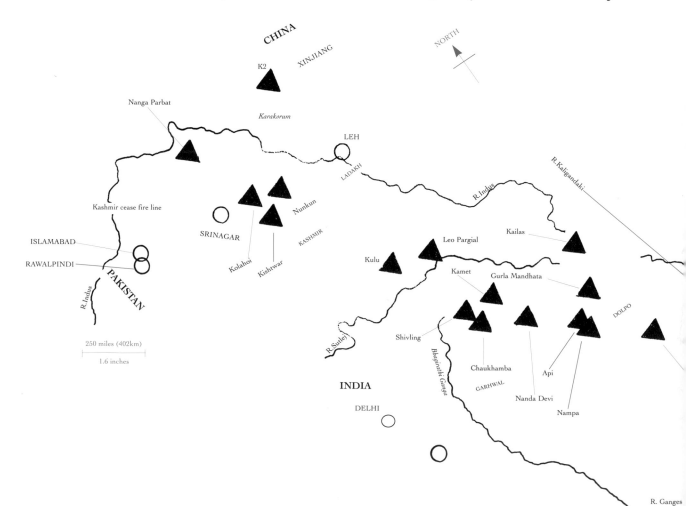

forested, are comparatively little known. Access to this politically sensitive region has been difficult for years, and although Bhutan is now allowing selected climbers and trekking parties to visit some its magnificent mountains, the Indian state of Arnachal Pradesh and Tibet beyond the watershed are strictly off-limits.

The high crest of the Kangchenjunga massif — the world's third highest mountain — divides Sikkim from Nepal. Its massed satellites include chisel-shaped Jannu (25,295ft/7,710m), and the celebrated view of 'Kangch' from the Indian hill station of Darjeeling affirms its local name 'The Five Treasuries of the Great Snows'. The circuit of the massif's western flank is one of the best treks in Nepal.

Many famous mountains, including four of the eight highest mountains (as opposed to summits), rise in the Khumbu, the region below Mount Everest and home country of the Sherpas. A land of neat villages, high open pastures and white peaks, it is, alas, for obvious reasons the most trekked area of the Himalaya, even boasting a regularly scheduled airstrip at 10,000ft (3,000m). Though the icy fang of Ama Dablam towering above the celebrated monastery of Thyangboche is a view familiar to many, the lovely valleys between Everest and Makalu are still wild and unfrequented.

A high glacier pass leads into the secluded Rolwaling glen over which, soon after the Chinese Road from Kathmandu to Lhasa crosses a low point in the watershed, the formidable double-headed Gaurishankar stands guard. Easily accessible from Kathmandu, the

**Jugal Himal and Langtang — Nepal, Tibet**
*Shisha Pangma (26,398ft/8,046m)*
*Langtang Lirung (23,769ft/7,245m)*

**Ganesh Himal — Nepal, Tibet**
*Ganesh I (24,298ft/7,406m)*
*Ganesh II (23,458ft/7,150m)*

**Gurkha Himal — Nepal**
*Manaslu (26,781ft/8,163m)*
*Himalchuli (25,896ft/7,893m)*

**Annapurna Himal — Nepal**
*Annapurna I (26,545ft/8,091m)*
*Annapurna II (26,040ft/7,937m)*

**Dhaula Himal — Nepal**
*Dhaulagiri 1 (26,795ft/8,167m)*
*Gurja Himal (23,600ft/7,193m)*

**Kanjiroba Himal — Nepal**
*Kanjiroba I (22,580ft/6,882m)*

**Yokapahar Himal — Nepal, Tibet**
*Api (23,399ft/7,132m)*
*Nampa (22,162ft/6,755m)*

**Gurla Mandhata Humla — Tibet**
*Gurla Mandhata (25,354ft/7,728m)*

**Garhwal East —India**
*Nanda Davi (25,645ft/7,817m)*
*Kamet (25,447ft/7,756m)*
*Changabang (22,520ft/6,864m)*

**Garhwal West ('Gangotri') — India**
*Chaukhamba (23,419ft/7,138m)*
*Kedarnath (22,769ft/6,940m)*
*Shivling (21,467ft/6,543m)*
*Bhagirathi I (22,493ft/6856m)*

**Punjab Himalaya — India, Pakistan**
*Nun (23,410ft/7,135m), Kashmir*
*Kun (23,250ft/7,087m), Kashmir*
*Leo Pargial (22,210ft/6,770m), Zanskar Range*
*Kulu Pumori (21,500ft/6,553m), Kulu*
*White Sail ('Dharmasura' — 21,148ft/6,446m), Kulu*
*Sickle Moon (21,570ft/6,575m), Kishtwar*
*Nanga Parbat (26,658ft/8,125m), Dardistan (Pakistan)*

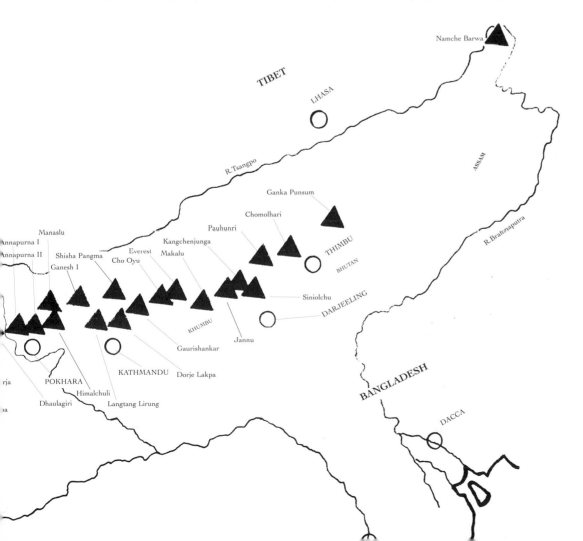

# THE HIMALAYA

superb peaks of the Jugal now cluster on the frontier adjoining the charming Langtang glen, a trekker's mecca. Part of the Langtang Himal, yet the highest mountain entirely in Tibet (and China), Shisha Pangma is the smallest of the 26,250ft (8,000m) peaks; its exact location was not pinpointed until the 1960s.

The deep gorges of the Trisuli and the Burhi Gandaki define the next range: the Ganesh, a group of daunting ice peaks well seen from Kathmandu yet rarely visited. The Trisuli is actually one of several rivers that rise north of the Himalayan watershed; draining the Tibetan plateau in ancient times, they cut their gorges faster than the mountains rose around them. And still they rise as the Indian and Asian tectonic plates continue their collision.

Dominating central Nepal, the proud white cone of Himalchuli is one of a small group of major peaks above the ancient capital of Gurkha. Another gorge system drains the hidden valley of Manang behind the ice-hung 30-mile (50km) rampart of the Annapurna Himal, from which rise 11 high summits and a score of lesser peaks. One of these, ethereal Machhapuchhare, is sacred and forbidden and must be the most famous mountain in the Himalaya after Everest. Just 21 miles (33km) separates the summit of Annapurna from Dhaulagiri, highest point of the next mountain group. Between the two, and 23,000ft (7,000m) below, flows the Kali Gandaki which rises in the desert-like trans-Himalayan kingdom of Mustang. The circuit of the Annapurna massif, traversing the Kali Gandaki gorges en route, is a justly popular trek.

# THE
# HIMALAYA

Behind Dhaulagiri is primitive Dolpo, where lies turquoise Phoksumdo Lake and where the mysterious Bon religion is still practised. Though opened to foreigners in 1990, access to this rugged region is difficult and there are few visitors. The same applies to far west Nepal where several impressive mountains and tranquil Lake RaRa, the largest of Nepal's only two sizeable lakes, are found, but the topography is complicated and communications difficult.

Abode of many Hindu deities, the lovely mountains of Garhwal stretch for nearly 150 miles (250km) from the Nepalese border and cradle the infant Ganges. With its splendid forests and flower-filled meadows, Garhwal has been compared to a scaled-up Switzerland and a network of military roads assist access to all but the still-closed Tibetan frontier region. Majestic Nanda Devi, rising from its almost inaccessible sanctuary, was once the highest mountain within the British Raj, while Changabang, an improbable tooth of white granite, is a remarkable neighbouring summit. Further west, lined by an avenue of savage summits, lies the great Gangotri glacier. Its remote snout beneath the stunning fang of Shivling is called Gaumukh and here the holy Ganges is born.

In the Indian states of Himachal Pradesh and Jammu and Kashmir a tangle of small mountain ranges collectively known as the Punjab Himalaya form a backdrop to the plains of the Punjab itself. Among them, twin-peaked Nun Kun is the highest but most mountains are considerably lower and the terrain is ideal for trekking and small expeditions climbing in alpine style: some excellent ski-mountaineering journeys have been accomplished. Especially notable are the jagged summits Kishtwar, Kulu with its shapely peaks and verdant orchards and the arid Zanskar Range. Historically the far western end of the Himalaya is part of the princely state of Kashmir, now disputed territory and isolated; ice-hung Nanga Parbat, the final mountain of the Himalaya, stands squarely in Pakistan. One of the world's great peaks, an aura of malevolence echoes its often tragic history. All the major summits of the Himalaya have now been reached, most of them many times. Commercial guided expeditions even attempt Everest and other coveted 26,250ft (8,000m) peaks, leaving the stage set for real mountaineering among the hundreds of smaller mountains that still remain inviolate.

# Langtang Lirung

IT had been a long day. We left our camp below the West Paldor glacier soon after dawn and found the high ridge of the Tiru Danda, along the crest of which our trail led south, still plastered in new snow. It was tough going for the heavily laden porters and for long sections the sherpas and I had to cut steps in the frozen snow fields and help them along. And then, just as the snow gave way to steep grassy downland, the mist came rolling in and visibility fell to just a few yards. Navigation was difficult, none of the sherpas had been that way before, and I had to think hard to recall exactly which of the network of shepherd's paths we had taken three years before in the sunshine and with all Nepal at our feet. Every boulder, every rhododendron bush, every looming tussock seemed familiar. By late afternoon there were rents in the mist and, resting against green banks studded with edelweiss and gentian, we caught glimpses of glittering icewalls to the north, the furrowed flanks of Pabil and Lapsang Karbo — the still-mysterious peaks of the Ganesh Himal. But we could not stop for long: we must find water and a place to camp before dusk.

It was already dusk and the mist was dissolving as we came to the narrow cleft of the Pansing Bhanjyang pass. Pemba's nose led us unerringly to a little alp hung on the eastern flanks of the ridge below the pass, where a stream tinkled down into the steep forest and a ruined stone-roofed byre built between two gnarled cedars gave us a comfortable night.

Eastward the alpenglow was already dying on the icy brow of Langtang Lirung, the great peak that dominated the horizon above the creeping night. The Lirung had been with us for almost the entire expedition; we had seen it from all angles, some ugly, some imposing, but it was never lovelier than now. The pink became purple, then steel grey and the day was finally dead. High above the mist-filled Trisuli gorges rode the silver moon. Night had come and it was time to switch off. 'Cha Sahib!' came a shout from the byre. 'Cha ready! Velly good cha!'

Jugal Himal, Nepal. *It is early morning near the Pansing Bhyjang pass on the Tiru Danda ridge. Langtang Lirung dominates the horizon while mist still fills the deep intervening Trisuli valley. Dome Blanc, Langshisa Ri and other peaks that cluster round the Langtang/Jugal watershed are seen in the distance on the right.*

Khumbu Himal, Nepal. *Mount Everest, known also as Chomolungma and Sagamatha, is seen with its surrounding summits. The photograph is taken from Mera Peak some 20 miles (32km) southward from Everest. The regular Nepalese route ascends the sunlit facet to the right of Everest's summit. Spiky Lhotse, at 27,940ft (8,516m) the fourth highest peak in the world, stands to the right of Everest while the long apparently flat-topped ridge on the left is Nuptse (25,850ft/7,879m) — the famous western cwm lies hidden between Everest and Nuptse.*

# Summit Reflections

WE'D been climbing steadily since dawn, Pin and I. Old chums, rarely needing to speak, we'd surmounted each obstacle with the fluency that comes of fitness and experience. In the early light we'd forced the steep face above the glacier. It was not high but it was hung with deep, cold and unconsolidated powder snow and climbing it was like grappling with vertical cotton wool. It was time-consuming, dangerous stuff and we were thankful to gain the lowest point of the ridge without a major problem. We'd traversed a sequence of small but knife-edge gendarmes and, cautiously moving together, had climbed a long and steepening snow crest. Intent on the business in hand, the exposure — that ever-deepening drop on either hand — had scarcely registered. Nor had we stopped to eat: a brief pause to snap a chocolate bar in two and we were moving relentlessly onwards again. Always the summit had remained aloof and the day slipped by unnoticed.

Eventually the crest ahead steepened into a nose of bare blue ice. It was my lead and, after a lengthy run-out, prudence took the upper hand — this was no place for a long fall. Balancing precariously on my front points, I gingerly tapped in a screw, wound it carefully home and clipped through the rope . . . Relax. Another bulge reared over me. Another screw at arm's length, this time for aid. An exploratory move . . . And then the big pull up and over. There was nothing above and nothing beyond. Just Tibet and a void of blue shadow. I turned to see the red ball of the sun dropping into a sea of misted hills. By the time Pin had joined me the last colour had fled westwards before the cloak of night and the tiny top was ours, our first proper Himalayan summit, ours alone in the darkness until the moon rose to share it.

When moonrise came in a couple of hours we could descend the east ridge on the far side of the mountain. Until then there was time to consider our situation, for our heady elation was laced with apprehension — that exciting what-if-it-doesn't-go? fear of the unknown. We had not expected to bivouac but surely we had no intention of descending the ridge we had climbed, certainly not in the dark.

Indeed that had never been our intention. On our reconnaissance from a distance, in daylight, we had selected the south ridge to climb because it looked interesting and was likely to be virgin, and the east ridge to descend because we supposed it to have been the route of the first — and only? – previous ascent. It had appeared straightforward though the very final section had remained hidden. But now that we knew the mountain first-hand we were not so sure; the report we had researched seemed not to fit the mountain we had climbed. What unpleasant surprises did the east ridge hold? Would it go by moonlight?

The darkness got colder and colder but the summit was small and no place to stamp around. We donned our duvet jackets and every stitch of clothing we had; we ate and mumbled and dozed. And then the moon, all but full, rose serenely out of the Langtang to bathe us in that ethereal light which renders every colour lifeless and every shadow black.

On reconnaissance, the top section of our chosen ridge appeared horrifically steep but we could abseil a couple of rope lengths down the moonlit face and traverse across a snow slope to where the angle of the ridge eased right back. We carried two or three disposable abseil tubes for such eventualities, sharpened two-foot lengths of old tent pole. No problem. It was good to be moving again. But once on the ridge things seemed different; in fact, rather hazardous. It was a condition we would come to recognise as characteristic of the Himalayan post-monsoon season: unconsolidated snow on northern faces and ice or hard nevé on southern slopes.

Traversing down that ridge, if not exactly difficult, was nevertheless heart-in-mouth climbing at its best. In retrospect we were in full control of the situation. Yet with a fathomless black void concealing deep steep powder snow on the left side of the narrow arête and ice glinting in the moonlight on the right side, I can well understand how we found the situation especially awesome at the time.

We led through, taking it in turns to lead, one of us always belayed. In the moonlight there was no end in sight — no safe place to aim at. For pitch after pitch, for what seemed an eternity, I inched crab-wise along the black shadow of the northern side, kicking my feet into the invisible snow, hands and axe picks clawing some sort of security in the ice over the knife-edge crest. At any moment I expected my unseen steps to collapse beneath my feet. Balancing meanwhile, on swiftly cut steps on the icy side, Pin would keep the rope tight expecting to check any fall with his weight and the drag of the rope over the crest. And it would probably have worked.

Eventually the crest widened and, with the moon higher in the sky, we could see both flanks of the ridge. Most of the danger was now past and there would only be hidden crevasses to concern us. Carrying coils, we moved together again, crossed over a couple of minor tops on easy snow slopes and then, there way ahead, we saw Windy Col. The tracks of our reconnaissance, distinct in the moonlight, led down from it and across the glacier towards our tent. It was midnight.

Jugal Himal, Nepal. *Gangchempo or 'Fluted Peak' seems to block the Langtang glen when seen from these yak pastures near Kyangjin Gompa. The upper glen is unfrequented, the scenery wild and the views spectacular.*

Kumbakarna Himal,
Nepal. *This is the formidable fang of Jannu (25,295ft/
7,710m) seen from the
Sinelapcha La as the morning mist clears. On the left is
Phole Sobithongje, a mere
21,880ft (6,673m) high.*

# THE HIMALAYA

Khumbu Himal, Nepal. *Tramserku (21,680ft/ 6,608m) is seen from an unusual angle rising high over the deep valley of the Dudh Kosi. Kangtaiga (22,240ft/6,679m) stands beyond. The view is eastwards from the high trail which links Thami village — where Sherpa Tenzing was born — to Namche Bazar, the Sherpa 'capital'.*

ABOVE: Ganesh Himal and Gurkha Himal, Nepal. *We sited Camp II on the remote east ridge of Himalchuli at 19,300ft (5,883m): this is the view looking over the edge close to the tents. The hanging glacier below is un-named while the clustered ice-peaks are the Ganesh Himal some 25 miles to the southeast.*

RIGHT: Garhwal, India.
*Dawn lights the awesome spire of Shivling and sweeps across the upper meadow of Tapoban (14,000ft/4,267m) to illuminate faintly the base camp of a climbing expedition. 'Shiva's Ling' is, of course, a sacred mountain and watches over the snout of the Gangotri glacier — Gaumukh (the 'Cow's Mouth') — where rises the holy Ganges.*

TOP RIGHT: Garhwal, India.
*Shivling — the summit pyramid is seen from Tapoban meadow in winter at last light after several days of continuous storms.*

Left: Kanjiroba Himal, Nepal. *The shapely peak of Kanchunne (c21,140ft/ 6,440m) rises over the glen of the Pungmo Khola as it climbs towards the Kagmara La, the high glacier pass linking the Phoksumdo Lake region of remote Dolpo with far west Nepal. It is early May and spring has yet to arrive at this altitude, some 13,000ft (4,000m), but the yaks must still be driven to pasture.*

Garhwal, India. *This is a different aspect of twin-headed Shivling, this time from due south across the Kirti Bamak in winter. The skier is approaching Camp 1 at about 17,000ft (5,200m) during a ski attempt on Kedar Dome, a rather higher peak than Shivling if rather more gentle on this, its northern flank.*

# THE
# HIMALAYA

ABOVE: Annapurna
Himal, Nepal. *Alpenglow
lights the imposing north-
western face of Annapurna I
here some 20,000ft (6,100m)
above the valley of the Kali
Gandaki near Kalopani,
shortly above the gorges
where this becomes the deep-
est valley on earth.*

RIGHT: Garhwal, India.
*The Sudershan Parbat mas-
sif rises to 21,348ft
(6,507m) to the north of
Gaumukh and is seen
reflected in a tiny tarn several miles southward — up —
the north-flowing glacier.*

Annapurna Himal, Nepal. *The remote and arid trans-Himalayan valley of Manang lies behind the Annapurna massif and is peopled by folk of Bhotian stock — ethnic Tibetans. This is a carved mane stone depicting Buddhist deities near Ongre village at about 11,000ft (3,350m). The complex north wall of Annapurna III rears up almost 14,000ft (4,267m) above the valley floor.*

# KARAKORUM &
# CENTRAL ASIA

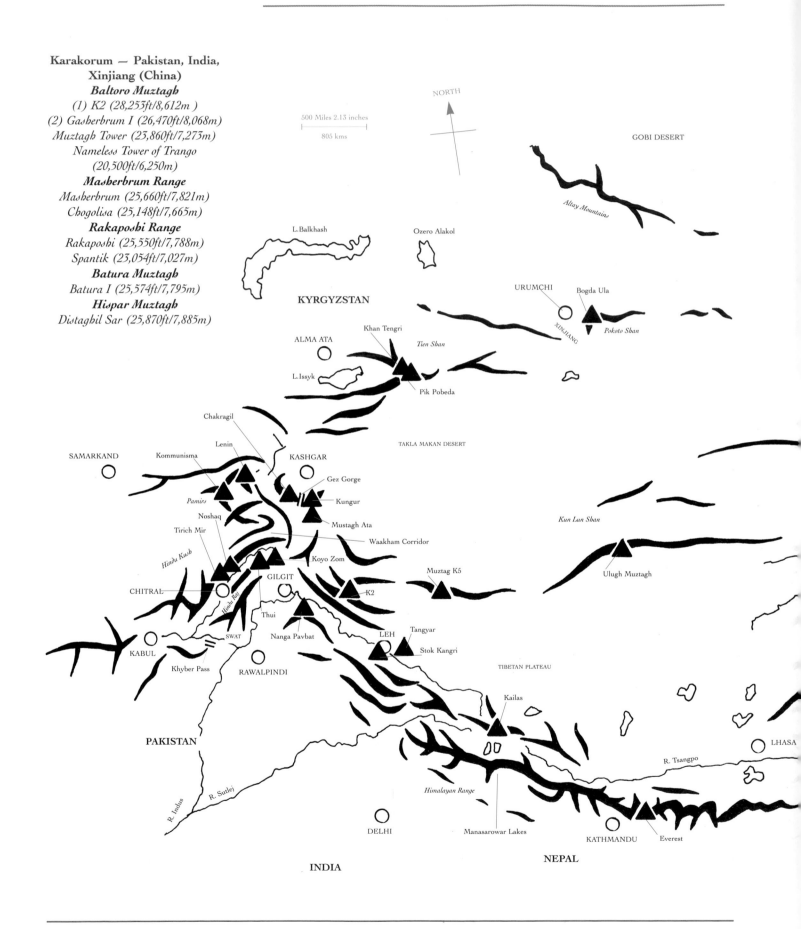

**Karakorum — Pakistan, India, Xinjiang (China)**
### Baltoro Muztagh
(1) K2 (28,253ft/8,612m )
(2) Gasherbrum I (26,470ft/8,068m)
Muztagh Tower (23,860ft/7,273m)
Nameless Tower of Trango
(20,500ft/6,250m)
### Masherbrum Range
Masherbrum (25,660ft/7,821m)
Chogolisa (25,148ft/7,665m)
### Rakaposhi Range
Rakaposhi (25,550ft/7,788m)
Spantik (23,054ft/7,027m)
### Batura Muztagh
Batura I (25,574ft/7,795m)
### Hispar Muztagh
Distaghil Sar (25,870ft/7,885m)

500 Miles 2.13 inches

805 kms

NORTH

GOBI DESERT

Altay Mountains

L.Balkhash

Ozero Alakol

URUMCHI

Bogda Ula

XINJIANG

Pokoto Shan

KYRGYZSTAN

Khan Tengri

ALMA ATA

Tien Shan

L.Issyk

Pik Pobeda

Chakragil

TAKLA MAKAN DESERT

Lenin

SAMARKAND

Kommunisma

KASHGAR

Gez Gorge

Kun Lun Shan

Pamirs

Kungur

Noshaq

Mustagh Ata

Tirich Mir

Ulugh Muztagh

Waakham Corridor

Hindu Kush

Koyo Zom

Muztag K5

CHITRAL

GILGIT

K2

Hindu Raj

Thui

LEH

Tangyar

Nanga Pavbat

SWAT

Stok Kangri

KABUL

Kailas

Khyber Pass

RAWALPINDI

TIBETAN PLATEAU

PAKISTAN

LHASA

R. Tsangpo

R. Indus

R. Sutlej

Himalayan Range

DELHI

Manasarowar Lakes

KATHMANDU

Everest

INDIA

NEPAL

Of the great fold mountains that radiate from the Pamir knot, we have already examined the Himalaya. Clockwise some 90 degrees, the next great chain — the Hindu Kush — stands beyond the Hunza river and the Indus. Initially running westward and then southwest, the Kush divides the plains of Pakistan from Afghanistan and the Turkestan deserts. It is an arid range where large mountains draped with sizeable glaciers rise over bare dusty hills, the parched valleys green only where irrigation permits. In the north and close to the anomalous Wakhan Corridor, created by the British Raj to keep the empires of Britain and Tsarist Russia at arms' length, the great mass of Tirich Mir is highest of the 20 summits which exceed 23,000ft (7,010m). It can be climbed fairly easily and, indeed, skied most of the way. Another group of interesting, but rather lower peaks, rises in Nuristan some 80 miles (130km) to the southwest. Entirely in Afghanistan these peaks provided challenging climbs to very small parties before the Afghan wars. The range rises again to the almost 17,000ft (5,200m) Koh-i-Baba massif 100 miles (160km) beyond Kabul before finally fading away into western Afghanistan. At the foot of Tirich Mir lies the deep and beautiful valley of Chitral, its eastern wall extending for nearly 150 miles (240km) as the Hindu Raj range, where several formidable peaks of similar style to the Hindu Kush rise above rather greener and more attractive valleys. Adjacent are the Trans Indus mountains of Swat and Kohistan.

Directly northward beyond the Wakhan, hard against the Chinese border and cradling the source of the legendary Oxus River, is the Pamir Range. Once entirely in the Soviet Union but now standing largely in Tajikistan, this is a great mass of high country some 200 miles (320km) square; the peaks, typically massive and icy, form roughly parallel crests between broad bleak valleys known as pamirs, peopled only by Tajik nomads and their flocks. Several huge glaciers, one of which, the Fedchenko, is over 40 miles (65km)

*Panmah Muztagh*
*The 'Ogre' (23,900ft/7,285m)*
*Saltoro Range*
*Saltoro Kangri I (25,400ft/7,742m)*
*Saser Muztagh*
*Saser Kangri (25,171ft/7,672m)*

**Hindu Kush — Afghanistan, Pakistan**
*(1) Tirich Mir (25,263ft/7,700m)*
*Tirich Mir East (25,233ft/7,691m)*
*(2) Noshaq (24,581ft/7,492m)*

**Hindu Raj or Trans-Indus Ranges, Pakistan**
*(1) Koyo Zom (22,546ft/6,872m)*
*(2) Thui I (21,850ft/6,660m)*

**Pamirs – Tajikistan, Kyrgyzstan**
*(1) Pik Kommunisma*
*(24,331ft/7,483m)*
*(2) Pik Lenin (23,406ft/7134m)*

**Tien Shan — Kyrgyzstan, Xinjiang (China), Kazakhstan**
*(1) Pik Pobeda (24,407ft/7,439m)*
*(2) Khan Tengri (22,949ft/6,995m)*

*Pokoto Shan massif, Xinjiang*
*(1) Bogdo Ula (17,864ft/5,445m)*

**Altay – Russia, Kazakhstan, Mongolia, Xinjiang (China)**
*(1) Gora Belukha (14,783ft/4,506m)*

**Chinese Pamirs or Kashgar Range — Xinjiang (China)**
*Tyube Tagh Shan*
*(1) Kongur II (25,325ft/7,719m)*
*Muztagh Ata massif*
*(1) Muztagh Ata (24,757ft/7,546m)*
*King Ata Tagh Shan*
*(1) Chakragil (22,071ft/6,727m)*

**Kun lun Shan – Xinjiang and Sichuan (China)**
*(1) Ulugh Muztagh*
*(22,628ft/6,897m)*
*Muztag — K5 — (22,014ft/6,710m)*
*Amne Machen (20,610ft/6,282m)*

**Ladakh Range – Kashmir (India)**
*Stok Kangri (20,082ft/6,121m)*
*Tangyar (19,626ft/5,982m)*

**Gangdise Shan or Kailas Range — Tibet**
*Kailas (22,028ft/6,714m)*

**Daxue Shan — Sichuan (China)**
*(1) Minya Konka (Gongga Shan — 24,790ft/7,556m)*

RIGHT: Pamirs, Tajikistan. *Mountains as far as the eye can see! This is the view southwards from the 24,551ft (7,483m) summit of Pik Kommunisma. In the mid-distance is the huge Fedchenko Glacier. This is savage country indeed.*

BELOW: Pamirs, China. *This is the western flank of the Kongur or Tyube Tagh Shan massif seen over Karakul Lake at 12,200ft (3,719m). A feature of the massif is the sequence of large parallel glaciers which pour down into the Ekki Bel Su pamir.*

long, pour down into the pamirs. Pik Kommunisma, a mountain of real Himalayan stature, was the old Soviet Union's highest summit and called Pik Stalin. Though not easy, it boasts nearly 20 different ascent routes. Comparatively straightforward, Pik Lenin is the world's most frequented 23,000ft (7,000m) peak.

Shipton, one of its early explorers, referred to the mysterious Chinese mountains just over the frontier as the Kashgar Range from the ancient silk road caravanserai at their eastern foot on the fringe of the Takla Makan desert. Though the Chinese conveniently include them in the nearby Kunlun to avoid any association with Russia, the most logical title for these mountains is the Chinese Pamirs. Hardly known to western climbers until the 1980s, they rise from high desert country as three groups, all hung with large glaciers. The two most extensive massifs rise either side of the impressive Gez Gorges, followed once by the silk road and now by the Karakorum highway. Highest is the Kongur massif, whose summit plateau remains above 20,000ft (6,100m) for some 10 miles (16km) and from which rise a series of high, sharp summits. Dozens of glacier tongues pour down into the desert. Muztagh Ata is a short distance south, a legendary mountain above the Silk Road whose massive summit displays huge walls to north and east but a fairly easy angled and glaciated western flank — it is probably the highest mountain to have been climbed and descended entirely on ski.

Stretching northeast from the Pamirs is the 800-mile (1,300km) crest of the Celestial Mountains — the Tien Shan — providing a

Hindu Kush, Pakistan. *Morning sun lights the great southern flank of Tirich Mir (25,263ft/7,700m) rising beyond one of the minarets of the mosque at Chitral.*

ABOVE: Chinese Pamirs. *Kongur II — the culminating summit of the Tyube Tagh Shan massif — is seen from the south over the pastures of the Su-baschi pamir close to the ancient silk road. This fine peak was first climbed by a powerful British expedition in 1981.*

RIGHT: Pamirs, Tajikistan. *A climber descends onto the summit ridge of Pik Kommunisma — the photograph is taken from the summit itself. In the far distance the peaks of the Chinese Pamirs are seen along the horizon.*

snowy backdrop to the great basin of the fearsome Takla Makan desert which it separates from the steppes of Kyrgyzstan. Though the region itself is arid, the highest peaks are concentrated in a remote area towards the middle of the chain where they rise above huge glaciers surrounded by beautiful forests and lush meadows thanks to the characteristic bad weather and heavy snowfall. Khan Tengri is a noble white pyramid while massive Pik Pobeda, second only to Pik Kommunisma in the old Soviet Union but actually astride the Chinese frontier, was not positively located until 1946. Eastward for 400 miles (650km) the Tien Shan lead into the heart of Xinjiang as bare rounded glacier-scattered hills of little interest before terminating in the small but lovely alpine massif of Pokota Shan, where several shapely snow peaks rise over forests and pretty lakes close to the Xinjiang's captial city of Urumchi.

The Kunlun Shan is another mysterious range, this time defining the southern limit of the Takla Makan desert which it separates from the Tibetan plateau, stretching from the Pamir Knot for 1,200 miles (1,900km) deep into China's Qinghai province. Rising from an already high plateau and thus displaying no great elevation, the loftier glacier-shrouded summits tend to rise as several widely separated knots. Muztagh — the term merely means ice-mountain — rises in the west just 300 miles (48km) from the Afghan frontier while Ulugh Muztagh stands 400 miles (650km) eastward on virtually the same longitude as Mount Everest. This is the highest peak in the range, a graceful two-headed pyramid encircled by gentle snowy satellites and surrounded by flat and featureless scree-desert. 600 miles (970km) further still, Amne Machen stands over upper reaches of the infant Yellow river.

Close to the Himalaya but not of it, the Gangdise Shan is one of several such crests in southern Tibet. Standing close to the remote Manasarowar Lakes where rise the Sutlej (Indus), the Tsangpo and the Karnali (Ganges) literally within a few miles of each other, Kailas is a holy mountain. Despite its unlovely sugarloaf shape, Kailas is considered to be the throne of Shiva and the centre of the Earth by the Hindu and Buddhist pilgrims, who measure themselves on the ground as they circumambulate it. In Sichuan, 1,000 miles (1,600km) eastward, noble Minya Konka stands on the far edge of the Tibetan plateau. An isolated and classic shark-fin of rock and ice it rises from an area of beautiful forests and meadows containing several smaller but interesting peaks.

One last range springs southeastward from the Pamir Knot. The Karakorum are high, savage and icy mountains which many consider to be the finest on earth. Comparable to but very different from the Himalaya — with which it is often confused — the Karakorum

# KARAKORUM &
# CENTRAL ASIA

*Karakorum, Pakistan. Small but formidable, the shapely peak of Bakhor Das (19,058ft/5,809m) presides over this view of the Askole valley near Chongo and above the great Braldu gorges. Thanks to liberal irrigation this part of the valley is comparatively lush — elsewhere it is an arid moonscape of scree and rock.*

is essentially an arid trans-Himalayan range, a rugged mountain desert virtually beyond the reach of the monsoon which so rules the Himalaya. Only high winter snowfall and constant irrigation make possible the scattered poplar-fringed oases resplendent with apricot groves, lush with barley, roses and wild lavender which characterise the deep Karakorum valleys. This complicated tangle of mountains and glaciers measures some 100 miles (160km) by 250 miles (400km) and from it rise a host of superb summits, typically tall angular ice peaks or savage rock fangs which are imposing, daunting even, rather than beautiful. They stand in avenues beside huge glaciers from which tumultuous rivers pour down to join the Indus or the doomed Yarkand, which dies in the Takla Makan sands. Nineteen Karakorum summits rise above 25,000ft (7,600m) while six of those clustering round the head of the Baltoro glacier exceed 26,000ft (7,900m) in height, including Broad Peak, the several Gasherbrums and K2, that great malevolent pyramid second only to Everest in altitude. Other well-known peaks lining the 35-mile (56km) long Baltoro are Masherbrum, the Matterhorn-like Muztagh Tower — it straddles the Chinese border peak as does K2 — and a whole cluster of amazing rock pillars such as the Trango massif's Nameless Tower, the Uli Biaho Tower in the Paiju massif and the delicate Lobsang Spires. Such improbable-looking summits are not rare in the Karakorum.

The Karakorum divides naturally into more than eight separate mountain groups divided by long glaciers, the longest of which is the Hispar/Biafo system which extends 60 miles (100km) snout to snout via the romantically named Snowlake. The Batura range beyond the Hunza river at the far western end of the Karakorum adjoins both the Hindu Kush and the Hindu Raj, while the far eastern area, the

Saltoro and Saser Muztagh groups beyond the 35-mile (56km) Siachen glacier, lie on the Indian side of the cease-fire line, a lingering manifestation of the still-simmering Kashmir dispute.

Access is difficult to this politically sensitive region. Indeed access to nowhere in the Karakorum is easy, though for different reasons. Naturally all travel is expeditionary but long arduous approach marches are the norm; there are few roads and no pack animals so everything must be carried by local porters who are unable to live off the country — the few settlements exist only in the lower valleys. Nevertheless the range is a mecca for climbers of all nations and strenuous if spectacular trekking is enjoyed up the great glaciers and over the many passes. While Himalayan alpenglow is a lingering pink, here in the Karakorum it is a flash of gold.

*Pamirs, China. A northern outlier of the Kongur massif, the 'Gez Matterhorn' (or Point 5,780m — 18,963ft) was so named by the British reconnaissance expedition of 1890. It rises over the arid Gez Gorge traversed by the Karakorum Highway and the ancient silk road en route to Kashgar and is a tempting goal for an enterprising small party.*

# The Roof of China

SHARP and mean, the wind sweeps across the roof of China. My windproofs flap incessantly as icy fingers probe between my ribs and chill the sweat on my back. I shiver involuntarily. We're on the summit at last. We've struggled for 18 hard days to reach this God-forsaken place. Yet it's difficult to feel elated. The job is only half-done. I know that I must not relax until we are all safely off the mountain. For I am expedition leader.

Colin and Grim crouch beside me on the little turret of black rock, the only finite point in a desolation of blowing snow and streaming cloud. Grim is a New England schoolmaster, Colin a heart surgeon from Nevada. Fumbling through four pairs of gloves I break a bar of Kendal mint cake, carried hopefully 10,000 miles (16,000km) for this moment. Colin grimaces beneath the surgical mask he is wearing, a novel protection against facial frostbite.

'It's an old English mountain goody,' I shout through the wind, 'Hillary and Tenzing ate some on the summit of Everest.'

Bob arrives. He is shouting ecstatically but his words are whipped away and lost in the void behind us. He removes his skis and struggles up awkwardly in his big boots to join us. Bob is an anaesthesiologist in Los Angeles. Now Johan approaches, head down as if to avoid the cloud that streams across the plateau so close above us. Another Californian medico, he's the veteran of the party and he skis in apparent slow motion. He's not fast but he's safe and very determined.

In the gap between the snow and the cloud I can see the white ramparts of the mysterious Kungur Shan to the north. The southern horizon is clearer, rimmed a hundred miles distant by the sawteeth of the western Karakorum — the frontier where once the Raj met Afghanistan and the empires of China and the Czar. Where once was played the Great Game. . . .

But this is not the time for reverie. At nearly 25,000ft (7,620m) the summit of Muztagh Ata is no place to linger. It's midafternoon and time to head down. The summit plateau is plastered with iron-hard sastrugi — plates of wind-blown snow 2-3ft (one metre) thick. Skiing across them is a penance and a sprained ankle now could spell disaster. But without skis we could not be here. Tingling with adrenaline I lead off towards the first of our bamboo marker wands, a black hairline against the white horizon.

This expedition I was leading was not the usual already close-knit group of climbing chums. Two years before Muztagh Ata had become the highest summit to have been ascended and descended, all the way, on ski — but by very accomplished mountaineers. A party of disparate if experienced ski-mountaineers, our party had come together for the sole purpose of repeating the ascent. I had been invited to lead the expedition and we had first met in Beijing. My responsibilities seemed daunting. Early on I had realised that any chance of success in the

inhibiting 21-day time slot allowed by the Chinese authorities would depend on proper altitude acclimatisation and my own logistic plan. We would adhere strictly to the old Himalayan dictum of 'climb high, sleep low', placing five camps at approximately 2,000ft (600m) intervals, expecting to spend three nights in each, meanwhile establishing the next camp above until just 1,700ft (500m) remained to the top. The main hazards would be weather and sickness; the major problems logistics and route finding — there are no sherpas to assist expeditions in China. Just arrived, we were unpacking the truck when an anguished American stumbled into our roadhead camp. He was leader on the expedition who had been trying the mountain a month ahead of us. Two men had disappeared going for the top and must now be presumed dead. The relaxed holiday feeling evaporated.

Twin-humped bactrian camels carried our gear across the desert to Base Camp where at 14,600ft (4,450m) our three Chinese staff kept house while we pushed up to the snowline and established Camp I close to where the massive skull and horns of a Marco Polo sheep — *ovis poli* — lay among the rocks.

It seemed incongruous to be skiing above a grey-brown landscape of dusty desert hills as we picked our

Pamirs, China. *Muztagh Ata: evening at camp III (20,900ft/6,400m) above most of the ice-fall difficulties. The view is to the southwest toward the high peaks of the Karakorum. Here we were pinned down for two days and two nights by a ferocious storm before we were able to push onward to camp IV.*

way through an ice-fall maze to pitch the four tents of Camp II in a snow bowl encircled by gaping crevasses. Safe from avalanche, the camp was close to the lip of an enormous precipice that promised the world's ski-jump championship to any careless navigator. Misty whiteouts completely obliterated our tracks as we climbed towards Camp III but this I'd anticipated and we marked the route with bamboo wands each marked with appropriate compass bearings. Then, at almost 21,000ft (6,400m), we discovered a lone tent in a hollow all but hidden by sheltering ice-cliffs. Full of food and gear, it was the abandoned top camp of our unfortunate predecessors and we added a second tent to establish our own Camp III.

That night the weather broke. For two days and two nights it stormed. Squeezed three of us into each two-man tent, we huddled in our sleeping bags, killing time by overhauling the black-smoking fuel-guzzling pressure stoves on which life depended. But for the food with which the abandoned tent had been stuffed we would have been hungry. It is at times like this that tempers fray, personalities crack and one learns the true measure of one's companions. Late on the second afternoon the weather eased and we looked out through the icicles to watch the sunset glow behind the Soviet Pamirs.

Now navigation was easy. It was straight up to the top. But it took over five hours to cover the next 2,000ft (600m) to where we had to cut platforms into the steep slope to pitch camp IV. Time was running short and I decided we should occupy after the second carry. But then the storm returned, this time far colder: we had little food and less fuel. We dozed and worried for a day and a night as the blizzard played wild music through the skis and poles stuck upright in the snow outside.

It was nearly dawn when I woke. The wind had died. We were enveloped in thick cloud. We brewed tea and dozed again. Suddenly it was 9.30am and the mist was streaming away under a blue sky. Go man, Go! But nothing is easy at altitude and it took almost two hours to put on our boots, scrape the snow from our ski bindings and get started. Though today we were skiing without loads, it took three interminable hours before the slope eased into a wide plateau with a turret of black rock on the far side and only space beyond.

Karakorum, Pakistan. *Last light lingers on the summit of Masherbrum (25,660ft/7,821m). The view is to the southwest from 'Bianje' on the Baltoro glacier. Masherbrum, one of the more striking of the higher Karakorum peaks, is the highest summit south of the Baltoro. After British attempts in 1938 and 1957 — the latter failing only 300ft (90m) from the top — Masherbrum was finally climbed by a strong American team in 1960.*

ABOVE: Karakorum, Pakistan. *This is an evening view down the Baltoro glacier from a camp at 'Bianje', a traditional site on a medial moraine near the glacier centre. Massed summits of the Paiju group fill the western horizon with the proud pinnacle of the Uli Biaho Tower (19,957ft/6,083m) prominent on the right. The Tower and Paiju itself (21,653ft/6,602m) were first climbed by an American and a joint US/Pakistani team respectively.*

RIGHT: Karakorum, Pakistan. *The trek up the Baltoro glacier is virtually a pilgrimage for any mountain aficionado. Sometimes the route follows lateral morraines; sometimes it takes the centre of the glacier. Always it is overshadowed by stunning peaks such as the Grand Cathedral and the Lobsang Spires — a mecca for ambitious modern rock-climbers..*

Karakorum, Pakistan. *Gasherbrum I (26,470ft/8,068m) stands in the innermost recess of the Karakorum. It was dubbed 'Hidden Peak' by Martin Conway in 1892 because it is invisible until the traveller has reached the one place on the remote Abruzzi glacier from which it is possible to gaze into its secluded glacier sanctuary.*

Karakorum, Pakistan. *Perhaps the great peaks of the Karakorum appear even more impressive by moonlight? This is a midnight view, a lengthy time-exposure of Chogolisa — 'Bride Peak' at 25,148ft/7,665m — and her satellites seen from the northeast at the junction of the Abruzzi and upper Baltoro glaciers.*

RIGHT: Karakorum, Pakistan. *Bullah Peak (20,650ft/6,294m) is one of the avenue of jagged summits which line the Biafo glacier. This view is from the south over the glacier's terminal moraines. The rose bush in the foreground may seem incongruous but such lone bushes are characteristic of the Karakorum and add unexpected colour to the harsh desert landscape.*

CENTRE RIGHT: Karakorum, Pakistan. *Sunset over the Upper Baltoro. This is the view from beneath 'Golden Throne' (Baltoro Kangri) northwestward toward Concordia. The twin summits of Mitre Peak (19,728ft/6,013m) rise on the left while the incredible fang of the Muztagh Tower dominates the horizon.*

BELOW RIGHT: Karakorum, Pakistan. *Beyond Paiju camp ground the snout of the Baltoro glacier, a great mound of rubble a mile wide, blocks the valley wall-to-wall, birthing the glinting skeins of the Biaho River. Campsites are few and far between here and expeditions are forced to camp at the same time-honoured spots such as Paiju. The improbable Trango Towers and the spires of the Grand Cathedral are seen on the left rising over the lower reaches of the glacier.*

Karakorum, Pakistan.
*The ancient fort at Baltit,
stronghold of the Mir of
Hunza and of strategic
importance during the play-
ing of the 'Great Game',
rises on the northern bank of
the Hunza River almost
opposite Takaposhi in the
western Karakorum. The
fine peak of Ultar II
(24,239ft/7,388) rises behind
the fort.*

# AFRICA

**High Atlas — Morocco**
*(1) Toubkal (13,665ft/4,165m)*
*(3) Jebel Ighil M'Goum*
*(13,356ft/4,071m)*

**Hoggar — Algeria**
*(1) Tahat (9,870ft/3,008m)*
*(2) Ilamane (9,050ft/2,758m)*

**Tibesti — Chad**
*(1) Emi Koussi (11,204ft/3,415m)*

**Mt Cameroon — Cameroun**
*(13,350ft/4,069m) — volcano*

**Simien Range — Ethiopia**
*(1) Ras Dashan (15,159ft/4,620m)*

**Ruwenzori — Uganda, Zaire**
*(1) Mt Stanley — Margherita*
*(16,763ft/5,109m)*
*(2) Mt Speke — Vittorio Emanuele*
*(16,042ft/4,890m)*

Africa is different. Of the 11.5 million square miles (30 million sq km)of the second largest continent, only a tiny proportion lies above 10,000ft (3,050m). It holds the least permanent ice of any continent; yet enigmatically the three small areas of glacier that do linger, do so astride the equator. Nevertheless Africa boasts some splendid mountains, many unlike anything elsewhere while scope for the exploratory cragsman is unlimited. In the following paragraphs we can touch only on the most important.

Most northerly of Africa's mountains, the Atlas extend for some 1,300 miles (2,000km) between the Mediterranean littoral and the Sahara desert, only in the far west rising much above 7,000ft (2,135m). Here the craggy knot of the High Atlas encompasses a dozen summits over 12,000ft (3,658m), none of serious difficulty. Holding heavy winter snow yet harsh and arid in summer, the range offers good rock climbing, often on granite, interesting skiing — both downhill and touring — and excellent trekking.

A thousand miles southeastward the isolated volcanic spires of the Hoggar rise from the desert. The spectacular aiguille of Ilamane is best known and since 1935 many expeditions have enjoyed steep and sensational climbing on the basaltic walls of this and other peaks. By contrast climbers have been disappointed by the impressive-looking cliffs of the several Tibesti massifs, long extinct volcanoes some 700 miles (1,000km) further east.

Much of turbulent Ethiopia is mysterious and mountainous — the largest area of high ground in Africa — and though most summits are accessible by mule the terrain is wild and huge cliffs and pinnacles await exploration by the dedicated cragsman.

A mere 20 miles (30km) north of the Equator rise the Ruwenzori, the legendary Mountains of the Moon. Claimed as the source of the Nile by Herodotus in 450 B.C., the range was unplaced for centuries until in 1876 the explorer Stanley glimpsed their distant snows. Standing in the Great Western Rift Valley and geologically block mountains, there are 11 major massifs, six of which hold small or tiny glaciers with 10 of the summits rising from them, characteristically plastered with bizarre ice formations, topping 16,000ft (4,900m). Despite typically poor weather, the higher peaks have been well explored and the best climbs are in alpine style on ice or mixed ground with a unique flavour. Below the peaks beautiful tarns lie in craggy valleys draped in weird afro-alpine vegetation — tree-heather and giant grounsel for instance — which provides a botanist's paradise. Access is easiest from the Ugandan side but is semi-expeditionary and for trips of any length requires the employment of local porters.

Isolated Mt Kenya, hung with 15 tiny and currently fast-shrinking glaciers, is Africa's most alpine mountain, standing virtually on

*(3) Mt Baker — Edward (15,889ft/4,843m)*
*(4) Mt Emin — Umberto (15,740ft/4,798m)*

**Virunga Volcanoes — Zaire, Ruwanda, Uganda**
*(1) Karisimbi (14,783ft/4,506m)*

**Mount Kenya — Kenya**
*(1) Batian (17,058ft/5,199m)*
*(2) Nelion (17,022ft/5,188m)*

**Kilimanjaro — Tanzania**
*(1) Kibo — Uhuru Peak (19,340ft/5,895m)*
*(2) Mawenzi — Hanz Meyer Peak (16,890ft/5,148m)*

**Mulanje massif — Malawi**
*Sapitwa (9,855ft/3,002m)*

**Chimanimani mountains – Zimbabwe**
*Inyangani (8,514ft/2,595m)*

**Namibia**
*Brandberg (8,550ft/2,606m)*

**Drakensberg — Lesotho, RSA**
*(1) Thabana Ntlenyana (11,425ft/3,482m), Lesotho*
*Injasuti (11,348ft/3,459m), RSA*
*Champagne Castle (11,072ft/3,375m), RSA*
*Monks Cowl (10,611ft/3234m), RSA*
*Cathkin Peak (10,390ft/3167m), RSA*

*Cedarberg*

*Hex River Range*

*du Toit's Kloof Mountains*

*Table Mountain (3,566ft/1,087m)*

*Mt Kenya massif seen from the northwest. From left to right: Tereri (15,467ft/ 4,714m), Point Lenana (16,355ft/4,985m) — with snow on it and the third highest summit of the massif — then Nelion and Batian (17,058ft/5,199m) the twin major summits, and finally the hump of Point Pigott (16,265ft/4,957m) to the right.*

# AFRICA

Kilimanjaro, Tanzania. *This is an early morning view from near the Barranco Hut at about 13,100ft (4,000m) of the southwest flank of Kibo, at 19,340ft (5,895m) the higher of the two principal mountain massifs that make up Kilimanjaro. The great Breach Wall — some 4,000ft (1,200m) high which has actually been climbed via its central icicle — is seen beneath Uhuru Point, the actual summit, (a point on the crater rim of Kibo) with the steep ice-falls of the Heim and Kersten glaciers, both serious climbing routes, to the right. The easy way up Kibo is hidden from this angle.*

# AFRICA

ABOVE: Ruwenzori,
Uganda. *The extensive
Stanley Ice Plateau crowns
the Mt Stanley massif and
the summits rise from it.
These are the two highest,
Alexandra (left — 16,703ft/
5,091m) and Margherita
(right — 16,763ft/5,109m).
Away to the northeast —
seen to the right, glacier-
hung Mt Speke is the second
of the Ruwenzori's six main
massifs.*

RIGHT: Kilimanjaro,
Tanzania. *It is late afternoon and the sun is already
low in the western sky. Cloud
fills the Western Breach —
in the crater rim — in this
view taken from above the
precipices of the 4,000ft
(1,200m) Breach Wall*

the Equator itself. Surrounded by a cluster of satellite peaks and easy of access, it compares well with the best of the Chamonix Aiguilles in the style and variety of the superb climbing it offers: there are no fewer than nine climbing huts surrounding the peak. The twin summits can be reached only by serious technical climbs but several of the lesser summits and the surrounding high moorlands, dotted with tarns and characteristic afro-alpine vegetation, provide excellent high altitude hiking.

The aloof and ice-draped cone of Kilimanjaro is a familiar safari backdrop. Kibo, the principle summit of this dormant volcano, contains a huge ice-choked crater from which glacier tongues cascade down its flanks. By its popular regular route, assisted by a sequence of modern huts and compulsory guides, the ascent is merely a straightforward if strenuous hike. Kibo's awesome southwestern flank however is remote and rarely visited and holds several long climbs on ice and poor rock of almost Himalayan style — probably the most serious on the continent. Eastwards across a high saddle rises the pinnacled crest of Mwenzi, the second peak, offering some worthy climbing on dubious rock and a stupendous east face — its ascent a most formidable undertaking.

Mountainous country rims the plateau that forms southern Africa. The Mulanje massif is the culminating point of an enchanting region of high moorlands and craggy summits where fine hiking and long rock climbs can be enjoyed. The Chimanimani of Zimbabwe have been well developed by local climbers and have been compared to the Scottish Highlands; however, uncleared mines — a legacy of the bush war — currently present an nasty hazard. Although comparatively small, the arid Namibian mountains offer intriguing possibilities. Perhaps best known is the Great Spitzkop — the Namibia Matterhorn — a spectacular granite spire that gives over 2,000ft (600m) of difficult climbing.

Hundreds of beautiful and shapely mountains form a broken chain of some 1,200 miles (2,000km) behind the eastern and southern coasts of South Africa. Highest are the splendid Drakensberg: scarp mountains with sculptured ridges, deep kloofs, proud pinnacles and frequent winter snowfall. There is good climbing but typically on poor basalt. Superb climbing on excellent sandstone and quartzite is found, however, in the south among miles of steep cliffs among such ranges as the Swartberg, the Cedarberg and the Hex River Range — fold mountains that for many miles front the interior plateau of the Great Karroo. In summer hot and arid, these mountains hold winter snow and there have even been ski developments in the latter range. Needless to say climbing, scrambling and mountain walking is a popular pastime and the Mountain Club of South Africa is extremely active.

Mt Kenya. *Point Peter (15,607ft/4,757m) is one of the many sharp satellites that cluster round the central summits. Its left skyline is the appropriately named Window Ridge, a very difficult rock climb. The view is eastwards over Oblong Tarn at about 14,300ft (4,300m) at the head of the beautiful Hausburg Valley. A specimen of giant tree groundsel* (Senecio keniodendron) *is seen in the foreground.*

# The Gate of the Mists

IT was a comfortable, if cramped, night. Nevertheless, I was thankful when the time came to start the brew. The Howell Hut — named after my good chum who built it single-handed in 1970 — is an incredible construction, magnificently sited but less than 4ft (1.25m) high and no place for a party. Jammed between the boulders at 17,000ft (5,182m) on the very summit of Nelion, it's a real port in a storm and has probably saved several lives not to say many unpleasant bivouacs.

We scrambled out and stretched in the dawn sunshine. Between the wreaths of mist that clung to the peak we could see buff-coloured moorland stretching away into blue distance. Africa. Though already on a summit, Batian, our objective — and Kenya's highest summit — was still ahead. Only 500 crow-fly feet (150m) separate the twin tops but the celebrated Gate of the Mists intervenes — a deep gulf which was already living up to its name. 'Weather's not too settled,' I said to my two protegees, 'so let's get cracking!' and we set off scrambling easily down the blocky ridge.

Before we dropped into the shadow, we marvelled at Brocken Spectres hanging in the mist below Batian's ghostly tower. It was the first time my companions had seen this phenomenon. Once on the shadowed northern side of the ridge — in January this is Mount Kenya's winter flank — we found everything plastered in verglass and spiky crystals of hoar frost. 'Look for a sling, fellows,' I called, 'there's supposed to be an decent abseil point somewhere around here.' We found it beneath the snow, and one by one the three of us abseiled easily down short walls and snowy ledges into the Gate itself.

The Gate of the Mists is the perfect col; a sharp ice arête curving between two rock buttresses not a rope's length apart. There's a great sense of exposure, for the glinting slopes either side drop steeply away into the abyss, or into fathomless mist as they did today. 'That's the top of the little Diamond Glacier,' I told the lads, pointing down to the left. 'Mackinder crossed it on the first ascent in 1899. Ollier and Brocherel took three hours to cut the steps. The ice was diamond-hard — so that's how they named it.'

'Where's the Diamond Couloir, then?' asked Steve. 'That's the famous ice climb here isn't it?

'Right below. Drop your axe here, it'll go down the Couloir.' I explained. 'Pin Howell and I had a couple of epics in it a few years ago. It's one hell of a climb!' Belayed by Chris, I cramponed carefully along the arête and found a good anchor on the far side — on Batian. We tied off the rope to aid our return across the Gate before Steve and Chris joined me. We tied on the second rope, scrambled round to the sunny southern side of the buttress and enjoyed the two pitches of straightforward muscular climbing on warm rock onto the flat-topped summit block.

Kenya. *Climbers watch the sunset on the summit of Nelion (17,022ft/5,188m), the slightly lower of the twin summits of the mountain. Batian, the higher top, is seen on the right — the Gate of the Mists intervenes.*

# AFRICA

RIGHT: Tanzania. *Ian Howell crosses the Silbersattel feature at about 17,500ft (5,300m) during the first ascent of the direct route on the hanging Kersten glacier on Kibo's south face. The Silbersattel is the only easing of angle before the summit ice-fields on this otherwise very steep climb, which necessitated spectacular aid climbing on a hanging icicle to surmount the lower rock band.*

RIGHT: Ruwenzori, Uganda. *The Ruwenzori are a botanist's paradise and the afro-alpine vegetation is quite extraordinarily luxuriant. This picture is taken on the shores of Lake Kitandara at 13,200ft (4,000m) in January in a tangled forest of Giant Tree Groundsel* (Senecio adnivalis) *and Lobelia* (L. wollastonii) *above a ground cover of Helichrysum* (H. stuhlmannii) *and rich mosses.*

FAR RIGHT: Ruwenzori, Uganda. *Abseiling into the ice cave at the head of the Savoia/Great Tooth Gully: the gully itself is a straightforward if steep descent from the Savoia massif to the Elena glacier but as in this case, the Ruwenzori cornices can be huge and can make such descents quite awkward.*

# ANTARTICA & THE PACIFIC RIM
# AUSTRALASIA

**New Zealand — South Island**
**Southern Alps**
*(1) Mt Cook (Aorangi —*
*12,349ft/3,764m)*
*(2) Mt Tasman (Horo koau –*
*11,475ft/3,498m)*

**Haast Range**
*Mt Aspiring (9,959ft/3,036m)*
*Mt Earnshaw (9,250ft/2,819m)*

**The Darrans**
*Mt Tutoko (9,042ft/2756m)*
*Mitre Peak (5,560ft/1695m)*

**New Zealand — North Island**
*(1) Ruapehu (9,177ft/2,797m)*
*(2) Mt Egmont (8,260ft/2,518m)*
*(3) Ngauruhoe (7,516ft/2,291m)*

Pride of place here must go to the noble mountains of New Zealand, among the finest and most important alpine peaks in the world. The 500-mile (800km) spine of South Island is entirely mountainous with dozens of summits topping 10,000ft (3,000m). Maritime mountains rising in the path of the prevailing Roaring Forties, they are characterised by the heaviest temperate-zone glaciation outside the Himalaya. Best known are the ice-hung peaks of the Southern Alps, the central section dominated by formidable Mt Cook, a mecca for international mountaineers and skiers. Of hardly less interest are other lower mountain groups to north and especially south, indeed a wilderness of jumbled mountains entirely fills the southwestern corner of the island. Of special note are Matterhorn-like Mt Aspiring and the Darran Range, which has been described as New Zealand's Bregaglia and includes much photographed Mitre Peak above Milford Sound. Climbing huts, long distance trails, excellent down-hill skiing and sympathetic National Park authorities ensure the popularity of mountain activities.

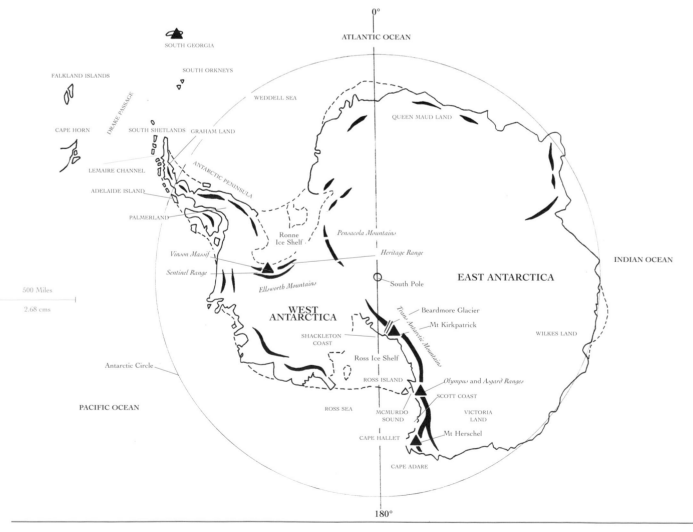

94

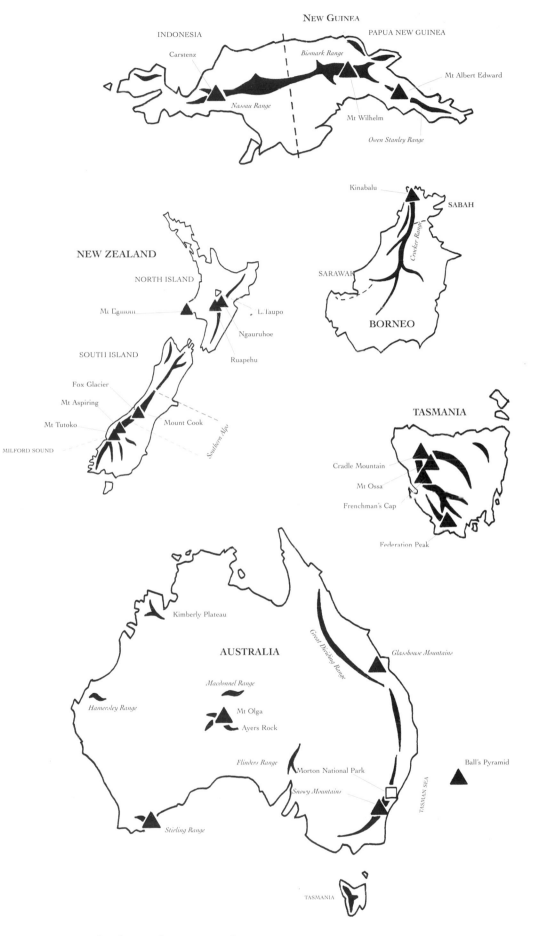

**Australia**
*Great Dividing Range/Snowy Mountains*
(1) Kosciusko (7,328ft/2,234m)

**Tasmania**
(1) Mt Ossa (5,305ft/1,617m)
Frenchman's Cap (4,734ft/1,443m)
Federation Peak (4,016ft/1,224m)

**Tasman Sea**
Ball's Pyramid (1,843ft/562m)

**Southern Ocean**
Heard Island – Big Ben
(9,006ft/2,745m)

**New Guinea — Indonesia & Papua New Guinea**
*Nassau Range*
(1) Carstensz Pyramid (Pik Jaya 16,532ft/5,039m)
(2) Ngga Pulu (15,945ft/4,860m)

*Bismark Range*
Mt Wilhelm (14,790ft/4,508m)

**Borneo — Malaysian state of Sabah**
*Crocker Range*
(1) Kinabalu (13,455ft/4,100m)

**Japan**
(1) Fujiyama (12,388ft/3,776m)

*Japanese Alps*
(2) Kitadake (10,472ft/3,192m)

**South Georgia**
(1) Mt Paget (9,564ft/2,915m)

**Antarctica**
*Ellsworth Mountains — Sentinel Range*
(1) Vinson Massif (16,864ft/5,140m)
(2) Mt Tyree (16,289ft/4,965m)

*Transantarctic Mountains — Queen Alexandra Range*
(1) Mt Kirkpatrick (14,800ft/4,511m)

NOTE: Islands not drawn to scale.

95

Flinders Range, South Australia. *This is the Flinders Range of South Australia seen from the west near Branchia on the highway up from Hawker towards Leigh Creek and the interior. The summits in the picture rise just above 3,000ft (900m) and the picture, with the characteristic gum trees in the foreground epitomises the small but shapely mountains of Australia. One of the country's better-known ranges, the Flinders is protected as a National Park.*

North Island is different terrain entirely with active volcanoes towering over its central uplands. Ruapehu is the highest; a great massif boasting a glacier-fringed crater lake and excellent skiing on its slopes. Ngauruhoe stands adjacent, a classic volcanic cone, while stately Mt Egmont rises above the ocean on the west coast.

By contrast Australia is barren and almost flat. Here are plenty of small mountains, though they are merely the eroded stumps of ancient ranges. The Great Dividing Range extends for 1,500 miles (2,400km) behind the east coast but it consists typically of high plateaux, fine cliffs and forest, exceeding 6,500ft (2,000m) only in the Snowy Mountains near Canberra. Here Kosciusko is merely the high point of a large area of attractive moorland and forest which holds a surprising amount of winter snow and offers excellent nordic and limited downhill skiing; there are several small ski resorts. Notable mountains elsewhere are the Flinders Ranges (c. 3,900ft/1,200m) north of Adelaide, the shapely Stirling Range (c. 3,600ft/1,000m) south of Perth and the bizarre towers of the Glasshouse Mountains (c. 1,800ft/550m) close to Brisbane. Tasmania, however, is a different matter, for here are real and very beautiful mountains with comparatively recent glaciation. Craggy summits, their approaches guarded by thick bush and often fierce weather, rise to around 5,000ft (1,500m) above tern-studded corries and invite some winter snow cover. Some long and serious climbs have been made in these exciting ranges.

Naturally 'bush walking' or 'tramping' is a popular activity all over Australia, as also is rock-climbing. Cliffs proliferate and provide climbs of as high quality as anywhere, which together with typically pleasant weather attract aficionados from overseas. Though big mountains are notably absent in Australia, expeditionary climbing of unusual style can be found on such features as Ball's Pyramid, a spectacular and difficult sea-mount rising sheer to 1,843ft (562m) from the Tasman Sea some 350 miles (550km) off Port Macquarie, and Big Ben on remote Heard Island. Technically this strange mountain is Australian territory though it rises 2,500 miles (4,000km) southwest of Perth. An entirely ice-sheathed dormant volcano just 12 miles (20km) across, its icy summit stands 9,006ft (2,745m) above an unfriendly ocean and its ascent is a difficult and serious undertaking.

New Guinea contains the third of the world's equatorial icecaps. Small glaciers and huge rocks walls are a feature of Carstensz Pyramid and its neighbours. The high mountainous spine extends for over 1,000 miles (1,600km) the length of the island but jungle and difficult access ensure that the mountains are rarely climbed.

Not so Kinabalu, by a huge margin the loftiest summit on the large island of Borneo and the highest point between New Guinea and the Himalaya. A mighty isolated and bepinnacled granite whaleback girded by titanic crags, it is climbed by hundreds of tyro climbers every year, assisted by two excellent mountain huts, well-maintained paths and ladders and no less than two miles of fixed ropes.

As might be expected of a major mountaineering nation, mountains and mountain activities are taken seriously in Japan. The ascent of Mt Fuji, the highest summit and one of 60-odd volcanoes in Japan, is an easy and crowded hike, but northwards 16 other summits rise above 10,000ft (3,000m) in the Japanese Alps proper. Here a succession of characteristically rugged and angular peaks linked by high and sharp ridges rise above steep forested slopes. Heavy winter snow lingers in patches well into summer. Excellent trails abound, there are many climbing huts and access is easy.

The Antarctic Continent is half as big again as Australia and contains several extensive mountain ranges. Once the sole preserve of official scientific and survey expeditions, since the mid-1980s well-heeled recreational visitors have been arriving in Antarctica in increasing numbers. Indeed, Vinson Massif, the continent's highest summit, is now frequently climbed by commercial guided parties. But access to most areas of the Antarctic is still impossible without major logistic resources while familiarity does little to blunt an extremely hostile environment.

Stirling Range, Western Australia. *The Stirling Range stands behind the coast near Albany in the far south-western tip of Australia. This is Bluff Knoll, at 3,520ft (1,073m) the range's highest summit. The regular ascent route, a steep and rocky trail, ascends the well-defined ridge in the centre of the picture but the large crags provide good rock-climbs here and on the other peaks in this rather peculiar range of upstanding and isolated mountains.*

# AUSTRALASIA

Southern Alps, New Zealand. *New Zealand's Southern Alps rise steeply from the wild west coast of South Island where in fairly recent times the Fox Glacier reached almost to the sea. This picture in evening sunshine was taken from near the little settlement of Fox Glacier in Westland National Park and shows (left) Mt Tasman (11,475ft/3,498m) and (right) Mt Cook (12,349ft/3,764m).*

RIGHT: Snowy Mountains, New South Wales. *The beautiful Snow Gum (Eucalyptus niphophila) is the symbol of winter in the 'Snowy'. This picture was shot about 6,700ft (2,042m) up during a nordic ski trip near the resort of Perisher in the Kosciusko National Park. At best Australian downhill skiing is comparable to that available in Scotland; serious enthusiasts adjourn to New Zealand.*

BELOW: Great Dividing Range, New South Wales. *Mt Carrialoo (2,251ft/686m) is not a single peak, rather a rugged forested plateau encircled by impressive cliffs. There is a definite wilderness flavour to the area.*

The Ellsworth Mountains stand at the base of the Antarctic Peninsular and here Vinson is surrounded by the sharp angular peaks of the Sentinel Range which rise some 6,000ft (1,800m) over the surrounding icecap. While the ascent of Vinson is merely a serious snow-plod, the narrow ridges and steep rock walls of Mt Tyree, Mt Shinn and other neighbours provide more formidable climbs.

Elsewhere the 1,200-mile (1,900km) chain of the Transantarctic Mountains virtually divides East from West Antarctica. Essentially coastal mountains, they extend above the Ross Sea shores, where the snow-free dry valleys of the Olympus and Asgard ranges are a notable feature, to the Ross Ice Shelf littoral, where as nunataks they peter out into the ice of the polar plateau some 250 miles (400km) from the Pole. Close to Mount Kirkpatrick, its highest peak, the Beardmore Glacier is the famous corridor through the range taken originally by Scott on his fateful journey in 1911–12

The peninsula itself, jutting well north of the Antarctic Circle and with its surrounding maze of islands, is entirely mountainous. The peaks, often spectacular and rising straight from the sea, are comparatively small and typically wall the inland ice-plateau. As the region most accessible to both insiders and outsiders over the years, much exploratory climbing has been accomplished.

South Georgia, technically a sub-Antarctic island and a dependency of the Falklands, on the same latitude as Cape Horn, is just 100 miles (160km) long and also entirely mountainous. Rather more accessible than the Antarctic itself, though with appalling weather, its shapely peaks rise from an extensive icecap and regularly attract hardy expeditionary mountaineers.

North Island, New Zealand. *Mt Ruapehu (9,177ft/2,797m) is an active volcano and the highest point on New Zealand's North Island with the popular ski resort of Whakapapa below its northern flank. Ski-mountaineers can ascend to the steaming glacier-surrounded crater-lake on the summit and return by one of several excellent descent routes back to civilisation. The picture shows a skier en route to the summit with the classically shaped volcano of Ngauruhoe (7,516ft/ 2,291m) in the distance.*

# The Murchison Amphitheatre

ONE more bounce and we were airborne, the rough grass strip dropped away and, climbing past the hamlet of Mount Cook, the Cessna headed up the wide flats of the Tasman River. Ahead the towering pyramid of Mt Cook itself filled the windscreen, the snow blowing from its summit, white clouds streaming into blue sky, supporting our reckoning that the storm was over. To exploit the weather slot we had decided to fly into the Murchison Amphitheatre, the expended dollars a fair exchange for a winter hike of some 25 miles (40km).

Banking over the three-mile wide (5km) confluence we turned into the deep trench of the Murchison. From our altitude of a few hundred feet, acres of abstract patterns covered the skeined flats below the glacier snout, each of the myriad channels outlined in snow. For four minutes we flew up the glacier, the steep white walls either side gradually closing in. Suddenly a spiky ice-hung crest blocked the horizon and we were banking steeply over a tangle of seracs tumbling into a flat-floored cirque. Wing down we made a couple of tight circuits, chasing our shadow round the Amphitheatre while Jim selected a landing site. He throttled back and we eased down onto the glacier, towing a snow plume from our skis.

Jim switched off the engine. 'There y'are fellas,' he said. We climbed stiffly down into calf-deep snow. Incongruous in the collar, tie and smart blue uniform of Mount Cook Airline , Jim helped us down with our awkward skis and bulging rucksacks.

'Thanks Jim,' said Collin, 'See y'around!'

'Mind how y'go fellas!' he replied before climbing back into the Cessna.

Taking-off in a cloud of spindrift, he waggled his wings and turned south, the sound of his engine fading as he disappeared into the glacier gorge. The silence was absolute.

'Bout seven-fifty feet uv' skinning up ter the hut,' grunted Collin, 'bit uv' a grind. '

'Then we'll have ter dig ter find the door — but then we'll put the kittle on!' declared Bill as we donned our skis.

Southern Alps, New Zealand. *In the winter dawn a ski-mountaineer crosses the Murchison Amphitheatre. The sun breasts the shoulder of Graceful Peak (c7,950ft/2,420m) while Mt Aylmer (8,550ft/2,606m) rises on the left. Both peaks stand on the Main Divide some dozen miles north-east of Mt Cook itself in the Mount Cook National Park.*

ABOVE: Southern Alps, New Zealand. *This is a winter view from the Tasman Saddle Hut at about 7,500ft (2,286m) southwestward down the great Tasman Glacier towards Mt Cook — seen in the distance at left. Mt Tasman is the rather more graceful peak immediately right of Cook.*

RIGHT: Ellsworth Mountains, Antarctica. *Climbers man-haul loaded pulques under the imposing walls of Mt Gardiner (15,380ft/4,688m) en route to an attempt on nearby Vinson Massif.*

LEFT: Ellsworth Mountains, Antarctica. *Near the summit of Mt Shinn (15,759ft/4,800m), the neighbouring peak to Vinson Massif. Its first ascent was made in December 1966 by a strong American party which also climbed Vinson and several other nearby peaks.*

BELOW: Transantarctic Mountains, Antarctica. *Elegant Mt Herschel rises in the Admiralty Range close to Cape Hallett in North Victoria Land.*

Spectacular rock obelisks guard the entrance to
the Lemaire Channel, a narrow strait between
the coasts of Graham Land (Antarctic
Peninsula) and Petermann, Pleneau and other
small off-shore islands. The voyage thorough the
Channel is one of the most spectacular passages
in Antarctic waters and several small peaks have
been climbed in the area.

# NORTH AMERICA

Greenland's magnificent mountains ring the edge of the vast ice-cap that covers most of this great island and rises centrally to 10,000ft (3,000m). The highest summit, Gunnbjorn's Fjeld, stands on the east coast but most peaks, often rocky aiguilles, are rather lower. The Staunings Alps further south have been much visited by climbers and a guidebook has even been published. Nevertheless mountaineering is expeditionary and approaches, especially on the sea-ice infested east coast, can be difficult, though stable weather during the short summer season and regular flights from Europe to the major settlements have made Greenland a popular goal for small parties. Regular air services also serve the settlements on Baffin Island enabling many small expeditions to explore among its jumbled mountains and icecaps. Big-wall climbs have been made on the spectacular ice-carved granite prows and spires of the Cumberland Peninsular while Mt Asgard, a pair of bizarre flat-topped pillars, must be one of the world's most peculiar peaks.

Mountains, many of them great and worthy ranges, occupy almost the entire western third of North America, sweeping down from Alaska to Mexico. Many of Alaska's fine

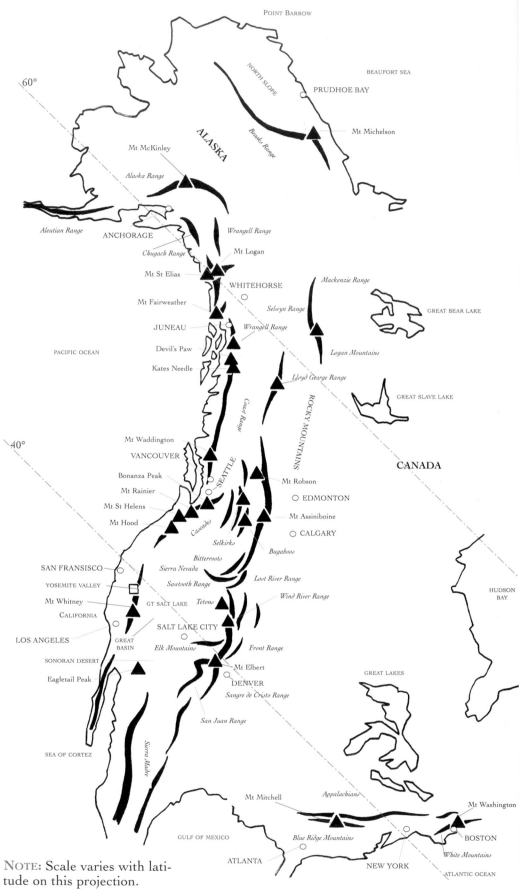

NOTE: Scale varies with latitude on this projection.

108

# NORTH AMERICA

ABOVE: Rocky Mountains, Canada. *This picture is taken on the banks of the Saskatchewan River close to the famous 170-mile (274km) Banff-Jasper Highway that traverses the heart of the Rockies — one of the world's most scenic drives. Beyond is Mt Amery (10,940ft/3,335m).*

RIGHT: Rocky Mountains, Canada. *Beautiful Mt Assiniboine is known as the 'Matterhorn of the Rockies'. It was first climbed in 1901 by Sir James Outram and his two Swiss guides. In this view from near Magog Lake the classic North Ridge falls toward the camera.*

South of the 49th Parallel, the American Rockies still define the continental divide but, unlike in Canada, they embrace many ranges of different character. Most extensive are the Colorado Rockies, where numerous branching sub-ranges form a sprawl of typically rounded and scree-covered peaks with occasional tiny glaciers lingering in their rocky corries. A total of 53 rise above 14,000ft (4,250m), most of them allowing very easy ascents. However there are several technically difficult summits and some excellent climbing — particularly in the Sangre de Cristo, Elk and San Juan groups, besides easily accessible crags near such cities as Denver and Colorado Springs. 30 miles (50km) from Boulder, Longs Peak in the Front Range is world famous for its big-wall routes.

Two particularly renowned ranges rise in the Rockies of Wyoming. The Wind Rivers are mountains for the connoisseur, 100 miles (160km) of shattered granite peaks running through a beautiful and remote wilderness. Eight northern summits top 13,500ft (4,100m) and hold small glaciers; more jagged peaks stand southward where such features as the Cirque of the Towers hold some of the best rock routes in the land. By contrast the Tetons, on a westerly spur from the divide, must be the most frequented mountains in the US. This small, compact and accessible group of sharp alpine rock peaks is dominated by the imposing Grand Teton; there are diminutive glaciers and a profusion of climbs. Not surprisingly the Tetons have played an important part in the development of American mountaineering.

Neighbouring Idaho is a largely wilderness state where the most important of its several ranges are the Sawtooths, a chain of granite aiguilles accessible from Boise, and the Lost River Range where Borah Peak is Idaho's highest. However these are branch ranges for the main crest of the Rockies follows part of the adjacent Bitterroot Range into Montana.

Following the Pacific Coast, the Sierra Nevada and the Cascade Range form the other great mountain chain that extends from southern California to Canada to become the Coast Range. Between this chain and the Rockies lies the Great Basin where arid mountains rise on occasion above 13,000ft (4,000m) and in Utah's Wasatch Range provide probably the most famous powder skiing in the world. However the region is best known for its deserts, where rise a host of sensational features such as Shiprock, Great White Throne and the Totem Pole besides other small but unusual mountains.

John Muir dubbed the Sierra Nevada the Range of Light. How very Californian! But large areas of bare white granite do indeed lend a rare quality to the light although the Spanish name might well describe the heavy winter snowfall. The Sierra stretch well over

# NORTH AMERICA

400 miles (650km) and the 11 summits above 14,000ft (4,250m) include Mt Whitney, the highest in the contiguous US, an easily ascended whale-back mountain of naked rock but boasting a superb bepinnacled eastern face. In summer snow patches cling to scores of jagged granite peaks that rise over craggy cirques where sometimes tiny glaciers still linger. There are a myriad tarns while meadows ripple with wild flowers. Characteristic is the steep eastern scarp of the range above the Owens Valley, one of the grandest mountain walls in the hemisphere, while the more gentle and heavily forested eastern slopes — famed for the big trees of Kings Canyon and Sequoia National Parks — are slashed in several places by profound canyons such as the incredible Yosemite Valley. Walled by acres of granite precipices, prows and pinnacles, and graced by beautiful feather-like waterfalls, Yosemite has become a tourist mecca as well as one of the world's foremost rock-climbing centres. El Capitan, a stupendous 3,000ft (900m) buttress, and the strange truncated hemisphere of lofty Half Dome, are the two best known features.

Two very different mountain types characterise the Cascades of the Pacific Northwest. A line of 10 major and several minor volcanoes, some extinct others such as Mount St Helens still definitely active, march northward from northern California almost to the

Rocky Mountains, Canada. *Bill March on the summit ridge of Mt Robson: this is the final crest above the so-called 'roof' at the top of the southeast ridge — the final section of the Kain Face route.*

Bugaboo Range, Canada. *The sheer west face of Snowpatch Spire (10,050ft/3,063m) rises from the snow plateau of the Upper Vowell glacier. The picture was taken from the prominent shoulder on the* voie normale — *the south ridge — of Bugaboo Spire, the name peak of the range, which we were descending after climbing its superb east arête.*

Canadian border. The highest, majestic and ice-hung Mt Rainier, dominates Seattle and the Pudget Sound landscape and offers a notable series of ice climbs of all standards — closely regulated by the National Park. It is certainly one of America's great mountains. In contrast the so-called North Cascades are the most alpine mountains in the contiguous US, a complex and rugged wilderness range of several hundred upstanding rock-peaks rarely topping 9,000ft (2,750m) but hung with ice fields and scattered with glaciers. The climbing here, on rock or ice, is of high quality but the weather is typically poor and many approaches are bedevilled by bush-choked valleys. On the peninsula west of Pudget sound stands the little Olympic Range, compact, heavily glaciated and reaching almost to 8,000ft (2,400m), these attractive mountains are known for excellent hiking and easy climbing.

In the east the Appalachians extend from Georgia to Maine, typically low, gentle and, except in New England, wooded to their summits. The range is famed for the long-distance Appalachian Trail that traverses its entire 1,200-mile (1,900km) length but good rock climbing can be found on scattered crags in many places. Of most interest are the White Mountains of New Hampshire where there is excellent rock on Cannon Mountain and serious winter climbing on Mt Washington.

Although there are large areas of rugged mountains in western Mexico, the continuation of the geological folds of the American Rockies, only rarely do they exceed 10,000ft (3,000m) and much detailed exploration is still to be done. The major attractions are the high volcanoes scattered across central Mexico. Citlalteptl is the third highest summit on the continent and together with neighbouring Popocatepetl is frequently climbed by snow routes.

# The Roof of Rockies

IT was a long slog up the Robson Glacier and, as the light faded, I began to wonder if we'd made a wise decision. It was the second time in 10 days we'd tried for Robson. The first time we'd hardly left the car park before the rain started. But we'd heard somewhere that the highest peak in the Canadian Rockies was also the most elusive; so, when the radio predicted a three-day slot in the typical Rockies' weather, we had to try again.

From the roadhead it takes all of a day to reach Berg Lake. When we got there, Robson looked so magnificent that we decided we wouldn't camp and waste 12 more hours, we would brew up, cache our unnecessary gear and continue climbing all night to maximise our slim chance of success.

In the twilight we reached the snowline and soon afterwards the base of the ice-fall. Here we were mystified to find a lone tent but no occupant. Roping up and now following vestigial tracks by the light of our head torches we started into the maze of crevasses and small seracs, constantly checking our general direction by compass. By alpine standards and in daylight the ice-fall would have presented no real problem but it was frustrating work in the dark and the poor snow made us wonder yet again if we were being stupid. Deep, soft and unconsolidated, it was obviously the result of the recent storms. Above the ice-fall we ploughed painfully up easy slopes on a compass bearing, every step a penance. Somewhere above was the Dome, a glacier knoll which we hoped we wouldn't miss. On it we'd planned to stop, brew up and doze for a couple of hours so that we could be on the Kain Face, supposedly the crux of our climb, with the dawn. But the condition of the snow now, when it should have been freezing hard, was worrying. 'If it's like this on the Kain Face I reckon it's a no-go,' panted Bill.

'It'll be crucifying,' I agreed, 'not to say an avalanche trap.' Out of the darkness ahead came a woman's voice.

'Who's there?' she called. 'Where are you?' shouted Bill.

'Up here, ah'll flash a light,' came the reply. We homed in on the voice and came to a roomy mountain tent. 'Ah' can hear you're Brits!' she exclaimed, 'Curm on in!'

We were as surprised as she was but there was hot coffee on the go and, as she plied us with goodies, Alison explained that this was the advanced camp of a party attempting to climb Robson by the Kain Face. Four climbers had left 20 hours before and had not yet returned. But there was nothing we could do except relax, imbibe Alison's coffee, swap gossip and enjoy our luck. The mountain world is a small one and we soon discovered we had American friends in common.

An hour before dawn and feeling well rested, we made preparations to leave but agreeing that if the snow was still bad when we reached steep ground we'd retreat. In some trepidation we ploughed up to the bergschrund only to discovered that the steep face above — all 800ft of the renowned Kain Face — was safe and the snow on it in a reasonable state. With crampons and two axes on we could kick decent steps all the way up. Unroped and following a line of old melted-out steps in the pre-dawn light, we climbed fast but before we reached the top figures appeared on the skyline and four men began laboriously to descend. We exchanged greetings as they passed but they were obviously exhausted after a long night out. The Kain Face led us onto an easy angled ridge where the full light of dawn, though watery and unpromising, found us in good spirits. If the weather held fair we must surely crack it?

Now on crisp snow we followed the ridge easily until it butted onto the steepening face that the guidebook appropriately dubs the 'Roof.' Here the crampon tracks of the other party abruptly stopped and we found the shallow ledge where they had passed the night. The roof, tiled as it were with ice-encrustations and small seracs, was fairly steep and very icy but quite straightforward if one selected the easiest line. So we put on the rope and moved together in regular alpine fashion. The Roof continued for nearly a thousand feet until it eased back into a crest of strange rounded cornices for all the world like gigantic curls of whipped cream.

Suddenly there was space all around and a strong feeling of height and exposure. Away to the left the crest reared up a couple of hundred feet into a sort of breaking wave formation and we made for it, giving the horrific cornices as wide as berth as we could.

The summit itself was perfect, virgin, an immaculate boss of hard snow. There was room for just one on the highest point in the Rockies. We took it in turns to stand there. Far below a rugged jumble of blue grey mountains spread into the distance, scattered with snow fields and scarred with black pine forest. Robson stood in fitful sunshine but streamers of dark cloud lay on the horizon and safe mountaineers are always mindful of the weather. And the descent.

But the descent proved swift and trouble free; we followed our ascent route but wore the rope to descend the Kain Face for the snow was already becoming dangerously slushy. On the Dome Alison was standing outside the tent.

'So you didn't make it?' she asked.

'Sure!' said Bill 'No problems!'

'But you've been gone only three hours!' she protested.

'Ah but it's a fabulous mountain and the going was good.'

'You Brits!' she exclaimed 'The guys have crashed out but how's about I make yer some breakfast?'

Rocky Mountains, Canada. *Mt Robson is the highest peak in the Canadian Rockies. Here it is seen from the north over Berg Lake into which the Berg glacier calves as miniature icebergs.*

# NORTH AMERICA

ABOVE: Rocky
Mountains, Canada.
*This is the final crest of
Mt Assiniboine's North
Ridge as it approaches the
mountain's fluted summit.
Bill March is unroped as
experienced climbers prefer
to be on straightforward
ground although we had
worn the rope on a couple of
awkward rock steps lower
down the ridge.*

RIGHT: Cascades, *Oregon.*
*An aerial picture of Mount
Hood, the fourth highest of
ten volcanoes that dominate
the Pacific Northwest.*

Yosemite, California. *Lost Arrow is the prominent pinnacle, free-standing for almost 200ft (60m) on the 1,400ft (427m) face of Yosemite Point. Its summit was first reached in 1946 by a rope traverse from the clifftop but its proper ascent by John Salathé and Anton Nelson the following year is considered a milestone in American climbing history. Upper Yosemite Fall beyond, at 1,430ft (436m), is the highest of the several spectacular waterfalls that grace the valley.*

# A Sonoran New Year

NEW Year is special. It's a time when a climber takes stock of the year's achievements and looks forward to new mountains and a season's fresh adventures. Indeed, much of the delight of mountaineering is either retrospective or anticipatory. But with luck New Year may be marked by some climbing of its own.

We met at a truckstop on Interstate 8 in the Arizona desert on New Year's Eve. We'd not met for several years and we dug into syrup waffles and milk shakes as we caught up on happenings. Then I followed his big pickup along the arrow-straight highway as the winter evening drew in. Eventually we turned off and stopped. The southern horizon, silhouetted black against a blood red sky, bristled with pyramids and pinnacles. 'That's the Eagletails man!' said Rusty, 'This is where we bivouac.'

We got a good fire going and cooked up the fierce chilli-con-carne that Rusty had brought from home. Then sitting in the sand we ate chocolate brownies and drank coffee, that special coffee that's brewed on an open wood fire. Then I cracked open my bottle of Glenmorangie. It was a decade ago and half a world away that we'd last enjoyed that together. In the flickering light of the flames the tall cactus stood over us like bizarre aliens, stepping ever closer each time we looked. And above us the Arizona heavens were ablaze with stars.

The Eagletails beckoned across the desert, the dawn light picking out every slab, chimney and crack of the spiky red wall. Choosing a low point in the wall we picked our way upwards over slabs, up gullies and in chimneys that never quite justified the use of the rope. And then we were scrambling along a rounded crest towards Eagletail Mountain itself, its twin summit feathers stark against the blue sky.

When we got there, we discovered there were actually three feathers, one masking another, each an imposing pinnacle rather more than 100ft high. One feather in particular appeared to lean right out over the southern precipice and the exposure, perched as the feathers already were at least 1,500ft above the desert floor, somewhat alarming. A single vertical pitch of serious muscular climbing led to each tiny summit.

All around stretched the moonscape of the Sonoran desert, harsh blue brown wilderness, much of it flat but much scattered with tortured eruptions of jagged rock which cast spiky black shadows across the desert floor. It was a chaos that begged to be explored but where water would be at a premium and the sun an enemy except in the dead of winter. Like now. It was an unusual place in which to welcome the New Year.

FAR LEFT: Eagletails, Arizona. *On the summit of Eagletail peak (3,304ft/ 1,007m) high above the Sonoran Desert.*

LEFT: Tetons, Wyoming. *The first snows of winter are captured in this mid-November photograph looking eastward up Teton Canyon above the valley of Pierre's Hole on the Idaho side of the range. The Grand Teton stands in the centre flanked on the right by Middle Teton (12,804ft/ 3,903m) and by Mt Owen (12,928ft/3,940m) — obscured by cloud — on the left.*

LEFT: Sierra Nevada, California. *The southern flank of Mt Russell (14,086ft/4,293m) rises over the cirque at the head of North Fork, Lone Pine Creek.*

LEFT: Yosemite back country, California. *Cathedral Peak (10,940ft/3,335m) is seen southward from Tuolumne Meadows up the valley of Budd Creek.*

# SOUTH AMERICA

**Serra Pakorima — Guyana, Venzuela, Brazil**
*(1)Neblina (9,840ft/2,999m), Brazil*
*Ayantepui (9,688ft/2,953m), Venezuela*
*Roraima (9,219ft/2,810m), Guyana*

**Brazilian Coastal Highlands**
*Serra do Caparaó Bandeira (9,462ft/2,884m)*
*Serra do Mantiqeira Agulhas Negras (Itatiaya — 9,255ft/2,821m)*

**Sierra Nevada de Mérida — Venezuela**
*(1) Pico Bolivar (16,410ft/5,002m)*

**Sierra Nevada de Santa Marta —Colombia**
*(1) Cristobel Colon (18,947ft/5,775m)*
*Simon Bolivar(18,946ft/5,775m)*

**Sierra Nevada de Cocuy — Colombia**
*Alto Ritcuba (17,926ft/5,464m)*

**Ecuadorian Andes**
*(1) Chimborazo (20,561ft/6,267m)*
*(2) Cotapaxi (19,347ft/5,897m)*

**Cordillera Blanca — Peru**
*(1) Huascaran (22,208ft/6,769m)*
*Alpamayo (19,510ft/5,947m)*

**Cordilera Huayhuash — Peru**
*Yerupaja (El Carnicero, 21,759ft/6,632m)*
*Jirishanca ('Humming Bird's Beak', 20,099ft/6,126m )*

**Cordilelra Vilcabamba — Peru**
*Nevado Salcantay (20,574ft/6,271m )*
*Pumasillo (19,915ft/6,070m)*

**Cordillera Urubamba — Peru**
*Nevado Veronica (19,042ft/5,804m )*

**Cordillera Vilcanota — Peru**
*Ausangate (20,906ft/6,372m)*
*Mariposa (c. 9,200ft/5,850m)*

**Cordillera Real – Bolvia**
*Illimani (21,201ft/6,462m)*
*Nevado Ancohuma (21,082ft/6,426m)*

**Cordillera Occidental — Peru, Bolivia**
*Nudo Coropuna (21,702ft/6,615m), Peru*

The narrow chain of the Andes stretching some 5,000 miles (8,000km) — the distance from London to Kathmandu — is the world's longest mountain range. Rising well north of the Equator, it plunges eventually beneath the cold ocean just 2,400 miles (4,000km) from the South Pole. It embraces many climatic zones, the world's largest area of equatorial ice, three distinct regions of active volcanoes as well as soaring rock needles and high altitude deserts. In places the peaks rise above the ruins of lost civilisations.

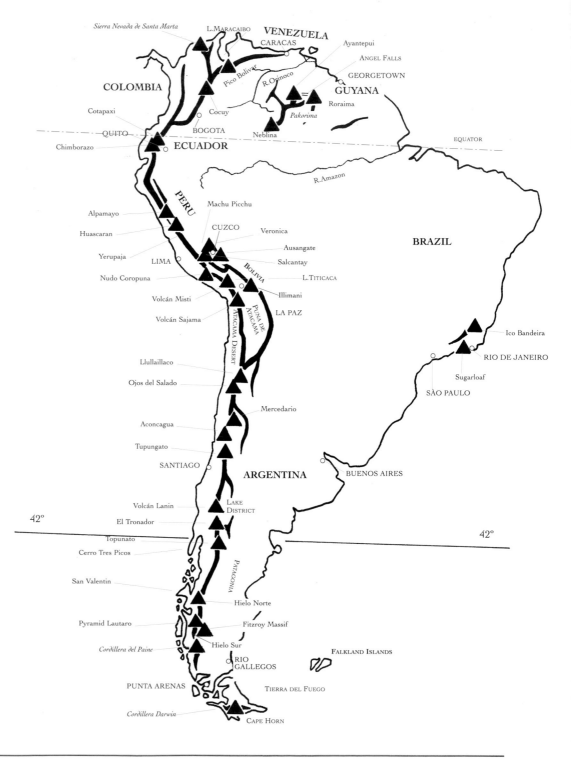

With two exceptions there is little high ground outside the Andes. One, diminutive by comparison, is the Brazilian coastal range behind Rio de Janeiro and the striking granite domes such as the famous Sugarloaf in the environs of the city itself. The other, far wilder and as strange as anything in the Andes, is the Pakorima Mountains between the Amazon and the Orinoco. This region of be-jungled lost-world mesas is the location of the world's highest water-fall (Angel Falls, 3,200ft/980m on Ayantepui) and the scene of at least one notable big-wall climb on Roraima.

The northernmost Andean range is the Santa Marta, a compact massif with pretty valleys and small lakes whose twin principal glacier-hung summits rise to almost 19,000ft (5,800m) just 30 miles (50km) from the warm Caribbean. Two other glaciated groups rise from the Cordillera Oriental, the eastern of the three Andean crests. The popular Merida is easily accessible from Lake Maracaibo while north of Bogota the misty Cocuy is notorious for bad weather. Ecuador however can boast arguably the world's finest cluster of volcanoes. Chimborazo, once thought to be the world's highest summit, and Cotapaxi, rising close to Quito and famed for its classic shape, are loftiest of more than a dozen volcanoes topping 17,000ft (5,200m). All are regularly climbed by straightforward snow/ice routes and there is an active local Club Andinismo.

As splendid as any on earth, the Peruvian Andes are the best known on the continent. Their fluted faces leaping from tortured glaciers, their ridges encrusted with wild ice formations, their cirques holding jewel-like tarns and rising from high pampas grass-lands: these are popular mountains for both climbers and trekkers. The weather is stable, virtually all summits have been reached and

*Volcán Misti (19,101ft/5,822m), Peru*
*(1) Volcán Sajama*
*(21,390ft/6,520m), Bolivia*

**Cordillera Occidental/Puna de Atacama — Bolivia, Chile, Argentina**
*(1) Ojos del Salado*
*(22,539ft/6,870m), Chile*
*Llullaillaco (22,057ft/6,723m),*
*Chile/Argentina*

**Cordillera Central – Argentina, Chile**
*(1) Aconcagua (22,835ft/6960m),*
*Argentina*
*Mercedario (22,211ft/6,770m),*
*Argentina*
*Tupungato (21,490ft/6,550m),*
*Argentina/Chile*
*Marmolejo (20,013ft/6,100m), Chile*
*Cerro Plomo (17,815ft/5,430m),*
*Chile*

**'Andean Lake District' — Argentina, Chile**
*Volcán Lanin (12,388ft/3,776m)*
*El Tronador (11,253ft/3,491m)*
*Volcán Osorno (8,728ft/2,660m)*
*Cerro Tres Picos (8,550ft/2,600m)*
*Puntiagudo (8,182ft/2,494m)*

**Patagonian Andes — Chile, Argentina**
*Hielo Norte San Valentin*
*(13,314ft/4,058m), Chile*
*Hielo Grande Pirámide Lautaro*
*(11,090ft/3,380m), Chile*
*Cerro Murallón (9,288ft/2,851m),*
*Chile/Argentina*
*Cerro Bertrand (10,560ft/3,218m),*
*Argentina*
*Cerro Fitzroy (11,171ft/3,405m),*
*Argentina*

Cordillera Blanca, Peru.
*Twin-headed Huascaran is Peru's highest mountain (22,208ft/6,769m) and together with the other peaks of the range it rises steeply over the long valley of the Rio Santa with its small corn fields, eucalyptus groves and neat villages.*

# SOUTH AMERICA

RIGHT: Cordillera Blanca, Peru. *Nevado Huantasan is a typical Blanca peak, sharp pointed and sheathed in fluted ice. In this picture it is seen from the Rio Santa Valley near the small town of Huaraz, the principle settlement in the valley and the nearest one finds to an alpine mountain resort.*

modern guidebooks cover the major ranges. Most extensive is the lengthy Cordillera Blanca where, of the 70 summits topping 18,000ft (5,500m), no fewer than 11 reach above 20,000ft (6,000m). But the highest peak, double-headed Huascaran, enjoys an evil reputation. In 1962 a hanging glacier breaking from its northern flank engulfed 6,000 people in a nearby village, while earthquake-triggered avalanches in 1970 destroyed Yungay killing thousands more. Fifteen miles (25km) northward stands the perfect ice-pyramid of Alpamayo, probably the most famous mountain in Peru.

Characteristic of the Peruvian ranges, indeed of the Andes, the Blanca is a narrow crest rather than the sea of peaks encountered in the Himalaya. In many places one can stand with one foot on the damp Amazon watershed, the other on that of the arid Pacific. In several places, however, there are small adjoining sub-ranges such as the Cordillera Ruara which rises behind the next group, the savage Huayhuash. Here a glacier tumbles into the tiny tarn of Laguna Niñococha at 15,580ft (4,750m), the hydrographic source of the mighty Amazon. Formidable Yerupaja and the Matterhorn of Peru, Jirishanca, are the most renowned Huayhuash peaks.

The Vilcabamba and Urubamba contain several fine peaks and rise on opposite sides of the Urubamba Gorge a short way downstream from that river's course through the 'Sacred Valley' of the Incas. The Vilcabamba is traversed in part by the ancient Inca Trail, the continent's most celebrated trekking route, which leads to the lost city of Machu Picchu perched on a ledge high over the gorge. Visible from Cuzco is the magnificent peak of Ausangate, a giant which dominates the extensive and beautiful Cordillera Vilcanota and the route encircling it a connoisseur's trek. With similar style but drier climate and higher snowline the next major group is the Cordillera Real, where icy Illimani towers over the Bolivian capital, La Paz, while a knot of slightly lower summits rises some 40 miles (65km) northward above the shores of Lake Titicaca. Meanwhile El Misti, rising over the charming colonial city of Arequipa, is best known of Peru's barren Cordillera Occidental, a sequence of high snow-tipped volcanoes which marches down into Bolivia where Sajama is that country's highest summit. This volcanic chain continues for nearly 1,000 miles (1,600km), forming the march between Bolivia and Chile and then Chile and Argentina. Its two parallel crests encompass the Bolivian Antiplano and the Atacama Puna, a waterless 12,000ft (3,650m) desert of salt flats and scree, second only to the Tibetan Plateau in altitude and extent. Among these lofty volcanoes is the world's highest, Ojos del Salado, currently dormant, but they are of more interest to the archaeologist than to the climber for pre-Spanish mummies and sacrificial remains have been discovered on several of their 20,000ft (6,000m) summits.

# SOUTH AMERICA

A scattering of volcanoes continues southward along the Andes almost to its end, but around latitude 30°S a lengthy chain of glaciated and more normal mountains reappears and is known as the Cordillera Central. Among its several lofty summits is the hemisphere's highest — massive Aconcagua. Ascending over interminable scree slopes, the regular route on Aconcagua is easy if gruelling. By contrast the intimidating ice-hung south face is 10,000ft (3,000m) high and its ascent a major mountaineering accomplishment. The mountain is easily accessed from the Argentinean resort of Mendoza and from Santiago, Chile's capital. This city is well sited for mountaineers with good climbing to be enjoyed on such nearby peaks as Marmolejo and Cerro Plomo while there are several nearby local ski areas.

Southward the mountains lose height but gain beauty and the 200 miles (320km) or so of the Lake District centred on the Argentinean resort of San Carlos de Bariloche is a popular and well-developed holiday destination. There is excellent climbing and skiing in the immediate Bariloche area where Cerro Tres Picos is the highest summit. Among other well-known Lake District peaks are popular El Tronador and the imposing aiguille of Puntiagudo and there are several shapely volcanoes.

The international frontier can be crossed on lake steamers. Beyond latitude 42°S stretches Patagonia, the final 1,000 miles (1,600km) of the continent where the mountains are ruled by both the west wind and the twin continental icecaps — the Hielo Norte and the Hielo Sur or Grande. The celebrated Californian climber Royal Robbins once explained that, while the weather rendered climbing in Patagonia sheer masochism, as a place to trek, photograph and experience it was second to none. Respectively 50 and 250 miles (80km and 400km) in length, the icecaps separate the storm-lashed

Cordillera Urubamba, Peru. *As one crosses the high puno from Cuzco northwards toward the valley of the Rio Urubamba, the Sacred Valley of the Incas, the peaks of the Cordillera Urubamba rise up like a wall ahead. Seen here is the major summit, Nevado Veronica (19,042ft/5,804m).*

fjords and beech forests of the wild west coast from the arid rolling pampas of the east. On both flanks great glacier tongues calve in large lakes or, on the west, often into the sea itself. Several volcanic peaks and rime-encrusted nunataks, among them San Valentin, Patagonia's highest point, jut from the icecaps both of which offer serious expeditionary ski traverses. However the most important mountains rise from the eastern and southern flanks of the Hielo Sur. Hard against the icecap and surrounded by the Argentinean Parque Nacional los Glaciares, Cerro Fitzroy and its serried satellites are among the most striking rock spires in the world, indeed Cerro Torre, the second highest, was long considered impossible and its eventual ascent generated much controversy. Entirely within a Chilean National Park, the Cordillera del Paine is a larger group enjoying slightly better weather. Several cirques of typically fang-like aiguilles dominate a lovely region of glaciers, blue lakes, primeval beech forest and flower-filled valleys that offers excellent trekking. Paine Grande is a formidable and rarely climbed rock and ice mountain but the group is famed for big-wall-type climbs on such peaks as the three Towers of Paine and the Fortress.

Beyond the Strait of Magellan, the mist-enshrouded and ice-hung mountains of the Cordillera Darwin suffer daunting weather but offer expeditionary climbs to those hardy enough to visit the area. In their rain-shadow lies beautiful walking country centred on Ushuaia, South America's final town.

Cordillera Vilcanota, Peru. *Dawn light gilds the characteristic cornices and ice flutings that guard the summit of Ausangate (20,906ft/6,372m).*

# To the Source of the Amazon

THERE is some confusion as to the exact source of the Amazon. The Americans favour the Apurimac, the longest of the headwaters, but the Royal Geographical Society prefers the Marañón which contributes the greater flow of water at their confluence and can thus be considered the senior tributary — the true hydrographic source. Though he had located the Marañón source himself some 30 years before, the veteran explorer Sebastian Snow was now unsure exactly where it lay. It was an obscure glacier-girt tarn the Indians called Ninõcocha somewhere behind the Huayhuash, he confided. Once in Lima with access to Alfredo's maps, I located a tarn of that name, vaguely fitting Sebastian's description, high in the Cordillera Raura, a minor range in remote country southeast of the Huayhuash.

The great ice peaks hid their heads in sullen overcast as we set off into the Huayhuash. The long narrow valley lay between arid grey hills and often we had to force our way through thickets of cactus beside the tumultuous river. At Llamac, the last village, a decrepit church, its mud walls cracked by earthquake, frowned down on the beaten earth of a rudimentary Plaza de Armas. Ragged children clamoured for candy and we drank beer at US$4 a bottle, a reflection of all 15 miles to the roadhead.

Next day we camped on the lush shores of Laguna Jahuacocha. The night was disturbed by thunder and the grumble of ice avalanches but the dawn was fresh. We were awed by the ice-hung walls of Jirishanca and Yerupajá now rearing close above us into a cloudless sky. The lakeshore was loud with birdsong; a heron stalked the reed beds and a gnarled Gueuña tree, bright with red blossom, overhung the turquoise waters. The next pass was steep and high — rather over 15,000ft (4,572m) — but we camped eventually in a valley filled with blue lupins and scattered with white limestone boulders.

Trouble arrived with the dawn. Two hombres in wide hats, their ponchos barely concealing big machetes, strode into camp. 'You have been fined 50,000 soles for passing through forbidden Quebrada Rondoy,' they announced.

To their surprise Alfredo, Peruvian but every inch an apparent gringo, spoke Quecha. 'How else are we expected to travel here from Jahuacocha?' he demanded. 'And how dare you ask for bribes! Your local magistrate will be interested to hear of this!'

*Cordillera Huayhuash, Peru. A team of burros, an expedition's logistic tail, crosses the bleak Punta Carhuac pass at 14,650ft (4,465m) at the northeastern corner of the range, well over onto the Amazon watershed. Behind to the southwest rises Jirishanca and, on the left, savage — and not so little — Yerupaja Chico (20,089ft/6,121m). It is interesting to compare this northeastern aspect of Jirishanca with that from the west (see next page).*

# SOUTH AMERICA

Their tone changed abruptly. 'You mistake us Señor, our village is obliged to pay for the upkeep of the trail. Any contribution from our honoured visitors would be welcomed.'

A round of face-saving bargaining ensured and eventually we donated 5,000 soles for 'path repairs'. 'Lone trekkers have been butchered for less up in the Blanca,' Alfredo shook his head sadly.

Condors circled lazily overhead as we climbed between towers of grey limestone to emerge onto a narrow crest between rocky summits. This was Cacanampunta, the continental divide at 15,400ft (4,694m) at the northern extremity of the Huayhuash. Dour grey-green hills stretched below us as we descended towards the Amazon.

Easy passes linking boggy valleys led us southward below the eastern ramparts of the mountains. At dawn not only Yerupajá, Peru's second peak also called El Carnicero, 'the Butcher,' but Siulá, Yerupajá Chico and Jirishanca itself, now warranting its Quecha name 'Icy beak of the hummingbird' were reflected in the mirrored surface of Laguna Carhuacocha. Now we turned eastward away from the big peaks, often following stretches of excellent trail that seemed almost to have been paved. One such section wound past dark tarns and into a narrow defile. It was an ideal place for an ambush. I could almost see the struggling band of weary conquistadores, their clothing tattered, their cuirasses rusted, suddenly surprised and slaughtered by screaming Inca warriors. But we were ambushed only by a ferocious hailstorm.

A tributary valley led us southward again and one night we pitched camp on a grassy ledge above a chain of little lakes over which a glacier snout hung below dark clouds. Was this the Cordillera Raura? The frosty dawn confirmed our assumption. Around us stood a semicircle of shapely peaks, pristine with new snow, rather smaller and more friendly looking than the savage Huayhuash. Now to find the Marañón !

We descended to another sizeable lake cradled by steep green hills. Icy summits stood behind. A peaceful river some 30 yards (27m) wide flowed from the lake between sandy shores. 'This is the Amazon,' declared Alfredo, 'at least it must be the Marañón!'

He pulled off his boots and socks and waded cautiously into the river. It was cold but not deep and we found a vestigial trail on the far side leading along the shore where two white stallions frisked in the long grass.

The next lake was smaller and the next smaller still, each linked by pretty waterfalls and cradled higher and higher into the green mountains. Beside Laguna Tinquicocha we paused to eat. I surveyed the far shore through my binoculars.

'That's odd,' I exclaimed, 'there's a ruined building above the head of the lake!'

'Ah-haa,' replied Alfredo, 'could be an old mine-working. There's a crossed pickaxe sign on the map somewhere around here.'

We climbed onward and upward. At length we rounded a rocky buttress and stopped in our tracks. Two stocky men in red helmets lounged against the fender of a huge battered yellow truck. A rough dirt road ended at our feet. An hour later we were holding on tightly as a similar yellow truck lurched to a halt in a cloud of exhaust smoke. Derelict buildings, cracked concrete and rusting machinery surrounded us. Oily puddles pitted the dirt road. A siren wailed and a series of dull explosions echoed round the sad mountains.

'Ziz is Mina Raura,' explained our driver proudly, 'ziz is most important zink mine in Peru.'

'But which way to Laguna Niñococha?' asked Alfredo impatiently. The driver pointed

'But Señor, why you want zat?' he seemed puzzled. 'Zat is ze reservoir for ze mine! Here we have ze taverna and ze house of pleasure . . . many nice girls . . .'

But we were already plodding up the trail.

We made our final camp at 15,560ft (4,743m) in a mossy hollow. Llamas grazed nearby but eyed us warily. The evening was clear and we walked the final few hundred yards to Niñococha — the 'Lake of the Child' — the source of the Amazon. A small concrete flood-wall barred the lower shore and a dilapidated hut full of valve wheels stood astride the infant river. Across the little lake a tongue of glacier curled into the grey-green water. Ironically, for the first time on our the journey we saw the alpenglow as it lingered on the small icy summits that surrounded this tragic place. Once it had been so very beautiful.

RIGHT: Cordillera Huayhuash, Peru. *The southwest spur of Jirishanca rises from the tortured Yerupaja glacier at the head of the Quebrada Jahuacocha on the Pacific — western — flank of the watershed.*

FOLLOWING PAGE: Cordillera Vilcabamba, Peru. *Last light on Nevado Salcantay (20,574/6,271m), highest peak in the Vilcabamba, a range on the east of the continental divide which feeds only the Amazon. The first western 'explorer' to visit the range was Hiram Bingham, the rediscoverer of the Inca ruins of Machu Picchu which stands on an airy ledge at the 'brow of the jungle' some 12 miles (20km) north of Salcantay. Indeed, this picture was taken from the Inca Trail which leads to Machu Picchu.*

# SOUTH AMERICA

RIGHT: Cordillera Vilcanota, Peru. *This fine line of comparatively small ice-draped peaks walls the Pachanta glacier on its northern side. Caracol, Concha and Pachanta all rise to around 18,500ft (5,639m), the first two names meaning snail and shell respectively.*

CENTRE RIGHT: Cordillera del Paine, Chile. *The Ventisquero (glacier) Grey, a huge tongue of ice nearly four miles wide, pours down from the Hielo Grande into Lago Grey at only 300ft (92m) above sea level. This is the smaller eastern of the twin snouts either side of a forested central rognon.*

BELOW RIGHT: Cordillera Vilcanota, Peru. *The Cayangate massif rises to several summits, Cayangate III — the central peak seen in this picture — seeming to be the highest top at about 19,400ft (7,915m). The view is to the southeast over the waters of Laguna Armaccocha, murky with glacial silt, at c. 15,000ft (4,500m).*

FAR RIGHT: Cordillera Vilcanota, Peru. *Here, rising above the head of the Quebrada Upismayo, is the huge northwest face of Ausangate, the monarch of southern Peru, a huge peak visible for miles around and the highest in the Vilcanota.*

ABOVE: Fitzroy massif, Argentina. *Cerro Fitzroy, hung with glaciers and surrounded by myriad satellite spires, is seen across the pampas from near the northern shore of Lago Viedma at a distance of some 45 miles.*

LEFT: Cordillera del Paine, Chile. *The incredible Towers of Paine are seen from the north near glacier-side 'Campo Whillans'.*

FAR LEFT: Cordillera del Paine, Chile. *The Towers of Paine rise over little Lago Torres in a bleak if extremely spectacular landscape of rock and retreating ice. The South Tower (left) is actually slightly the higher of the trio; the more impressive Central Tower was first climbed in 1963 by a British party which included Don Whillans and Chris Bonington*

# SOUTH AMERICA

PREVIOUS PAGE:

LEFT: Fitzroy massif, Argentina. *Wild flowers in the rain in the rugged western cwm of Loma de las Pizzarras are watched over by one of the spiky Dolomite-like sub-peaks of the Techado Negro — typical of Fitzroy's lower satellites.*

RIGHT: Fitzroy massif, Argentina. *Despite the awful weather that assails the Fitzroy region, the foothill country below the snowline is attractive in an unusual way. Primeval beech woods, moody tarns, lowering skies and tantalising glimpses of snow and spires through the mist reward hikers hardy enough to accept the frequent storms. This picture shows the valley above Laguna Hija with the Loma de las Pizzarras on the left.*

THIS PAGE: Cordillera del Paine, Chile. *A rainbow, a frequent occurrence in Chilean Patagonia, plays round a southern summit of the Cerro Ohnet massif (c. 5,000ft/1,500m) rising over the deep glen of the Rio los Loros where it enters Lago Dickson.*

RIGHT: *The mighty whale-back of Kinabalu (13,455ft/4,100m) in the Malaysian state of Sabah is the highest point on the large island of Borneo. Above the treeline the mountain is hung with crags — some of them quite prodigious — and paved with granite slabs from which rise several summits and many bizarre pinnacles. The pair is known as the Donkey's ears and Tunku Abdul Rahman Peak lies beyond: a very singular mountain indeed.*

PREVIOUS PAGE: Cordillera Vilcanota, Peru. *A stormy night with new snow ends in a lurid dawn behind the small yet fierce peaks of Tinki (17,880ft/5,450m — left) and Caracol (18,435ft/5,619m) west of the Pachanta pass, a glacial passageway through the centre of the range.*

RIGHT: *Kitadake (10,472ft/3,192m) in the Southern Alps of Japan is the second highest mountain in the country, overshadowed only by the famous volcanic cone of Fujiyama. This picture taken on a cold winters dawn from near Kitadake's summit shows Fuji in the distance, some 35 miles (50km) away to the southeast.*